The Common Sense of Teaching Reading and Writing

Caleb Gattegno

Educational Solutions Worldwide Inc.

First published in 1985. Reprinted in 2010.

Author: Caleb Gattegno

ISBN 978-0-87825-184-1

Educational Solutions Worldwide Inc.
2nd Floor 99 University Place, New York, N.Y. 10003-4555
www.EducationalSolutions.com

Table of Contents

Foreword

A cursory look at the Table of Contents will show that in a common sense review of the problems presented by reading we have to begin with those presented by the spoken language. We must understand the latter in the light of what it can contribute to a more organic and more dynamic insight into what might help those students who are attempting to master reading.

It has been a constant surprise to this writer that teachers of reading are quick to object to each other's concerns with the challenge of reading and rarely invoke the need to put all their cards on the table before entering a discussion. In this book, we shall depart from this custom and spell out every one of the premises we are conscious of, so as to eliminate deliberately sources of confusions. The words: children, reading, writing, comprehension, skill, etc. will not be left unqualified and readers will know all the time which of their meanings are being considered.

The bibliography at the end of the book is not intended to serve readers as usual reference lists do. Since in the story of my work,

I have found myself to be a lone investigator engaged on an untrodden path, unattractive to others, I do not find it appropriate to quote many writers besides those who have either worked with me over the years or have worked on some attributes of my contribution.

A universal approach to learning to read exists which applies to all languages, but because of the singular fact that I am writing in English (and will presumably be read mostly by people whose language is English) I might generate for my readers both some tensions and some valuable openings. The tensions will result from my having in my mind what perhaps cannot be evoked by some readers; and the openings, from the fact that native users of English do not spontaneously benefit from the exposure to writers looking at reading as a set of challenges wider than those presented by English alone.

In this foreword, I can restate that I am not a "reading specialist." I came to the field of reading by accident at the end of 1956 and had not by then read seriously a single paper on the topic. My own background as a self-taught scientist and mathematician prepared me in only one sense for such a study. That was, to let the challenges educate me so that I produce the instruments for reaching truth as it presents itself in this field. In fact, I had and still have no ax to grind. I am, as a scientist, only concerned to speak about what I consider to be the truth in the matter. My readers must judge me mainly on whether or not I have departed from this imperative.

Coming to reading from mathematics and the exact sciences, I have asked questions which sound very strange to reading specialists: "What is the role of algebra in reading?" or "What does the temporal component of speech contribute to the act of reading?" This means, that I was at once vulnerable to the presence of algebraic operations in the demands of reading and of time, as an important component of speech.

In the late fifties and early sixties, when I enquired of reading specialists about ongoing research on these two aspects of reading, I only heard that none of them knew of any such study. This dearth of fundamental basic research in this field was confirmed by friends looking at the literature, including the most recent publications.

So, in this book readers may encounter their first exposure to these matters but written from the point of view of the *Common Sense of Teaching*. This means that if they are concerned with the basics in that field, my findings will be of great help to practitioners in their classrooms everywhere. This is a rare attribute of the academic research going on in education.

My experience as a teacher of reading over only twenty-five years — all over the world and in a score of languages — permits me to say that what I learned was done in the presence of learners and checked against their progress. I often was challenged by very "hard cases" (as they were introduced to me); by large groups or by individuals, often badly traumatized. I developed ways of diagnosing what was required and I devised ways of meeting individual needs. I still do. The field of teaching is for me at the same time a field of research. I know that every one of my findings is empirically founded and does not represent an a priori theoretical stand. I know in particular, that I am ready to reject some of my present views, based on the facts I met this far, and to replace them by new ones when new facts impose themselves. This is the only attitude a scientist can adopt: "temporary evidence leads to temporary views" and *this* is a permanent maxim.

In this book, only indirect reference will be made to the *subordination of teaching to learning*, although it is part and parcel of the expression of what is being presented to teachers in these *Common Sense* writings.

After twenty years and more of presenting this approach to teachers, I may be permitted to take it for granted that readers will try to see whether it is actually part of every example worked out in the text.

* * *

In serving teachers through this book, I hope to serve students who do not need to pay more than it costs to acquire the ability of using another form of their own language in the way they used the spoken one, and of developing the intrinsic powers of the new form which do not belong to the first.

When they learned to speak, children gave themselves the entry into the oral traditions of their culture plus the means of relating to others on matters of day to day life. When they master reading they give themselves the key to the domain of the literature in their own language and all the expanse of experience beyond them which they can now live vicariously. When they reach a certain level of mastery of writing they can give permanent form to their feelings and to their thoughts, to the flights of their imagination, and conceive of affecting the course of human evolution as countless others did before them.

Reading and writing can become as much the birthright of everyone as their speaking has always been. Accepted by all, the last one is not disputed, we can make the first two as easily acceptable since their cost, in time and energy, is made as small as we know it can be.

To this task I dedicate this long study.

P.S. There is one part of learning to read which is considered in the body of this book and concerns itself with giving learners the ability to scan a text and sound its words in the manner those who can read do. This includes components of decoding, of phrasing and fluency which makes reading almost equivalent to speaking the text for the benefit of the hearers. Comprehension would also be included when the subject matter and the vocabulary are familiar to the utterer.

In September 1972, an alternative to the way to read shown in this book, came to me and I called it "*Infused Reading.*" Because it appeared that the vast majority of non-reading people (who are neither deaf nor blind) will not be able to escape knowing how to read by that way of acquiring the complex process, the word *infused* suggested itself.

Since the summer of 1981, thanks to the power of the microcomputer, it has been possible to produce at a reasonable price, diskettes which give the skills above at an unbelievable speed. Tested again and again, *Infused Reading* can now be offered as a valuable alternative to the most successful approaches devised to date. Hours are sufficient where until now months (and exceptionally weeks) were considered the norm.

The rest of the work forming the language arts area, has not been given the same form as yet.

If you own an Apple II+ or *e* or *c* computer, you have a chance to check the above personally.

P.P.S. Work done in the early seventies on teaching reading to the deaf, led to a program on film (silent) called *"Absolute Visual Reading"* still available. A manuscript for the series *"The Common Sense of Teaching . . . the Deaf"* was completed around that time but is not yet published.

A simpler and more functional approach to teaching reading to the blind was proposed in 1980 under the name *"A New Braille."*

For more information write to the publisher.

Caleb Gattegno
New York, 1984

Introduction

After twenty-five years of experimentation into the field and a study of a number of problems met by students of reading in a few languages and by their concerned teachers, I come to write this book which aims at bringing some common sense in the field.

It seemed necessary, to the scientist in me, to cast my net as widely and as deeply as I could so that every element of importance in the challenge is not left out.

There are languages written without capitals, others without punctuation, others with signs representing syllables and vowels; some arranging their words above the line while others hang them under the line; some arrange them vertically others horizontally; from right to left or from left to right; some use only consonants in their writing but imply vowels; some use characters and others letters or clusters of letters, some attempt to keep one sign for one sound, others do not mind to allow extreme ambiguities to persist.

In spite of this variety, countless numbers of people all over the world learned to read and write to various degrees of proficiency. Some people learn to read before they are three, others only in their old age, others find it extremely difficult to master reading and give up their attempts quite early in their school careers, while others manage to make sense of it after some clinical sessions; there are even some people who learn to read after they learned to write or rather, design the statements of their written language (which seems perhaps reasonable where hieroglyphics or ideograms are used for writing).

Hundreds of thousands of people must have given some thought to the challenges of reading and writing and the literature in the field is so broad that, most likely, there is no one alive today who can hold in mind all the details of those many studies. New challenges are constantly being added and investigated, making the overall survey of the field constantly more difficult.

In this book, the approach is that of common sense. It is the study of the challenge of reading and writing as met by humans conscious of that dimension of humanity called awareness.

If it is mostly specialized (in parts II to IV) in the case of the English language, this is because no one has the task of teaching just reading to humans but many have that of teaching reading a specific written language to those who already know how to speak it — in this case English — (and in other publications Amharic, Arabic, French, German, Hebrew, Hindi, Italian, Japanese, Mandarin etc.).

We still devote Part I to knowing the challenge in human terms and particularly to the exploitation, for the benefit of acquiring reading, of the remarkable job of learning to speak, which almost all of us manage in infancy.

Much more could be written about the theme of Part I — and some will appear as part of the book *"The Common Sense of Teaching the Deaf"* — but enough is included here to assist in the very specific and technical matters involved in teaching reading and writing to English-speaking people. As an illustration of the general approach, English is a sufficiently broad example.

* * *

Part I is about learning in general and learning language in particular. Much of what appears here is either hinted at or developed in my text "*In the Beginning There Were No Words; The Universe of Babies*" written to help parents understand the enormous powers of learning of very young children and see to it that they are kept alive ever after. Of course, teachers and psychologists who are parents may draw still more out of this text because of their professional interests.

Teachers of reading will mainly find that the powers which help babies crack the code of the language spoken around them can be used to crack the written code much more easily than is usually believed.

Hence, they can expect that their students can decode their language very quickly, in some cases merely in a few hours.

Once decoding is behind them, reading gains new dimensions, and teachers can then engage in widening their students' mental powers by introducing them to challenges in the language field which cannot be met on the fleeting medium of the spoken language although they are present there too. For example, making students aware of word orders; of structures, syntax, spelling, styles, selection of words; of changes of some words from one grammatical category to another according to the context; of key words such as prepositions, because of their constant reappearance in statements, etc. etc.

It is most likely that this abundance of new tasks — accessible when language is written and possibly left untouched when a language is only spoken — has made teachers say that learning to read is a much bigger challenge than learning to speak (finding confirmation of this thought in the known fact that although most children learn to speak there are many who fail to learn to read). Still a few moments of reflection will make plain how difficult the task of learning to speak one's native tongue, spoken in the environment, is. Besides being fleeting and disappearing forever unless one picks it up from the air, and holds it in one's memory, respecting

1 the sounds in each word,

2 the order of these sounds,

3 the stresses in those with more than one syllable,

4 how some merge and others don't,

5 how intonation affects them,

6 how to retain long strings of them,

7 how to make sense of what one has heard,

there is another component of the spoken language which tells us much about babies' use of their intelligence in this apprenticeship, and it is considered now.

In the environment, one only hears voices. These differ in pitch and timber and every baby must ignore these characteristics in order to reach the energy of the sounds which go to compose the words. How would a few months old baby tell itself that such objective physical components as pitch and timber, *are not the ones* to be taken into account and *that instead* the (arbitrary) choices of far smaller amounts of energy (which are used to create the individual oral words) form what it must focus on and integrate them in one's voice before they are carried to others?

That we all did it spontaneously, so early and in general, so adequately, is the marvel of that learning. It deserves our respect and our attention. It would make us into better observers of babies and infants and of their very able learning in so many fields. Then only, shall we be prepared to understand that the first steps of reading can be made so simple and can be owned almost at once by very young children. Making sense of the act of reading can be immediate. This will help in tackling the numerous other tasks which are now possible on the written materials. The replacement then in the curriculum of the word "reading" by the expression of "language arts" is justified.

The above paragraphs can be read as an attempt at removing ambiguities in circulation among people who use the word "reading" but who may be using it without ascertaining its meaning first. In this book, Chapter 7 is devoted to the complex task of finding what can be understood when the word reading is used by anyone. We believe these distinctions may have very salutary effects in the circles where reading people (specialists, consultants, supervisors, teachers) operate. To know that there are *a score* of meanings for such a current word — many of which are used very widely but not with the required precautions — may reduce the time wasted in public quarrels and in this case, restore some precision badly needed.

* * *

In keeping with the above, we introduce from the start four meanings of reading and devote Part II to their exposition.

"R_0" is the set of exercises which give newcomers to reading the required *discipline* as defined by the statement, "Let each word tell you what to say."

"R_1" takes the discipline of "R_0" to the stage where letting the words tell what to say produces English statements. A great variety of them is possible, in spite of the restricted choice of signs which trigger a restricted number of sounds.

"*R2*" extends "R_1" to the complete set of the sounds of English. If English had been written in such a way as to let each sign trigger only one sound and conversely, "R_2" would have completed the job of giving students a written code for their spoken language. But it is not the case, and there remains a task which is completed in "R_3."

"R_3" is "R_2" extended to include *all* the spellings used in English so that anyone can write correctly all one can say.

In fact, this is *our definition of literacy.* Those will be deemed literate who can write all they can say within the limits — however extended or restricted — of their vocabulary and their mastery of structure, and of spelling.

To ask for more would be legitimate only if we *all* accepted that the definition be applied to us as well. To go beyond the true relativity above would lead us to an absolute for which no one would qualify. Indeed, the sciences and the many specialized studies of art, music, sport, etc., have created kinds of slangs or dialects, and in such numbers, that no one could master them in one lifetime. Much that we can witness from a distance does not trigger in us any meaning for those statements which may seem natural to the specialists in their fields.

We are clearly all only literate in narrow areas of human endeavors and hence are illiterate in the others. This is not very helpful, but it militates in favor of our definition.

Hence, "R_0" to "R_3" make people literate.

To go beyond we need to educate ourselves. In this book, only after classifying the score of meanings of reading available do we treat one of them more fully. We chose "R_4." "R_4" is the application of "R_3" to *the acquisition of knowledge* through the use of the written language. This is important today, because the written word is still the main vehicle for the transmission of knowledge for which schools and universities are built. "R_4" is truly economical if we want our culture to continue and to make progress, one generation after the other.

Part III of this book, contains, besides the two chapters just mentioned (7 & 8) one on spelling (6). As far as we know, it is the first time such a complete study of spelling has been made available to so many teachers and their millions of students who only before were introduced superficially to the challenge that has been imposed on users of the written English language since the time of Chaucer. That chapter is divided into two parts, one studies the problems of spelling and the other gives numerous exercises which take care of these problems and can be deemed a solution.

* * *

Part IV is dedicated to writing.

For years, workshops and seminars on the learning and teaching of writing have produced a great deal of material which could fill a number of chapters. But we resisted that temptation and we only concern ourselves here, with a few aspects of the challenge as it appears to school people.

In one chapter, we develop approaches which link writing to saying and therefore take care of the source of all writing; *having something to say*.

In the next chapter, we take a close look at *the attributes of writing* which require the attention of all those who must use writing as a medium for their own expression. Expression can be linked to so many of the developments in the medium during the last few centuries — and particularly, in the democratic societies of our modern world. If reading has been expanded in spite of the phenomenal growth of the visual media, it implies that there has been an equivalent expansion of writing.

In the last chapter of this part, a study of genre and style in relation to the teaching of writing will attempt to put every reader in contact with the sources of both, thus opening new vistas for the future of the education of the creative writer in each of us.

Part I

Language Learning and the Place of Reading

1 Languages and Language Learning

No one will dispute that every language we know of started as a spoken language and much later, either spontaneously among its users, or artificially by outsiders, it was committed to a spatial or written form.

No one will dispute either that all of us first learn our mother tongue as an oral instrument of expression, and only later, may be exposed to the written language and need to learn to read.

No one will dispute that the spoken language is a fleeting reality carried by a multiplicity of voices in the environment and must be extracted from these in order to be reached per se. Hence, learning to speak draws us as babies to a very definite intellectual activity involving every one of us in the complex job of extracting words from the vehicles that carry them.

No one will dispute that while voices transfer energy from speakers to hearers, and therefore constitute an accessible reality in which the energy distribution may relate to the expression intended, words themselves do not share such a property. Words are arbitrary sound clusters, as one can immediately be sure of if confronted by a foreign language one never heard.

No one will dispute that the meaning of words is not a primary reality. Meanings are inferred through a complex process involving perception, association, abstraction, retention, testing and finally adoption of words as triggers in context and for specific reference.

No one will dispute that words alone do not constitute a language. Their various groupings, their functions in such groups, the stresses in them, the melodic lines that link them, are also part of the reality confronted by everyone who considers language as a whole and as an instrument of expression.

No one will dispute that, while each of us is born in an environment where one language (at least) is spoken — born not knowing it and having to acquire it — the language has become part of the environment through a complex historic process. We are therefore facing a dual challenge: on the one hand, we have to understand how the successive generations in a group come to produce a language which is adequate for the purposes it has been created for, and on the other hand, how each member of the group in subsequent generations penetrates the existing complex and makes it his or her own. No one will dispute that the two processes differ radically although they may be linked in a number of ways.

* * *

These points being conceded on the basis of common sense we can consider for a moment whether we can reach a definition* of language which is helpful in our efforts at understanding the creation *and* the adoption of a language by any group.

We shall endow a certain number (unspecified but larger than two) of humans with one attribute: awareness. This is a most primitive reality. Every reader will know at once that he or she has it. Indeed, awareness is that property of one's self which ascertains that one is, at this moment, reading these words.

Because I am writing on this day, I shall allow myself to use terms that I know to be current and are as meaningful to my readers as they are to myself. For instance, when I say, "perceptible reality" I do not think anyone would ask of me to include these words in a glossary. Likewise, if I said that a sentence spoken corresponds to a certain energy distribution over its duration, no one will ask for explanations.

I shall assume that every one of my readers knows —

1 that the system of cells, tissues and organs of a person alive (which we call one's soma) is capable of energy exchanges at physicochemical levels (which we also call biological),

---

* In the optical sense, i.e. so that one can say: "I see! I see!"

2 that that system is integrated so as to be known as one's own, responding to one's will, receiving energy but also capable of sending some out, and that one can be aware — at least sometimes — of such energy transactions,

3 that our sense organs are specialized receivers organized biologically to carry on functions to which we give names such as seeing, hearing, smelling, tasting, touching, etc.,

4 that we can activate or deactivate some of the sensory functions — particularly when we sleep — and that the activations may have been given special names as in the case of listening and looking (though not in the case of all the other senses),

5 that such activations may be accounted for by the presence of oneself in the activity.

Perception will be used here to account for the presence of the self in some activity leading to awareness both of the self and of the activity. Specialized perceptions are possible because of the existence of differing somatic terminals found in the sense organs and the brain.

To live, generally speaking, is coextensive with processing energy.

Humans can become aware of their own perceptions and of the differences between these. We shall add that perception, as we see it here, is the source of truth for the individuals concerned.

Awareness that one is perceiving is synonymous to knowing truth through that perception.

Human beings endowed with awareness of their perceptions, are capable of operating on the awarenesses of any of their inner perceptions and because of that alone, can produce a universe which is clearly manmade. What is singularly human then is that within the self, two realities can be reached through awareness: one is the processing of impacts on the soma of energy received, and the other, concomitant with the first, is awareness of the processing of energy. The self aware of the latter can focus on it and find in it what escapes when one only concerns oneself with the processing of energy.

For the purpose of inventing a language there is only need for this dual awareness and this justifies the old definition of man as an "animal owning language."

Indeed, we need to be aware that we can perceive at the same time some definite thing as we perceive a definite sound and the simultaneous awareness produces the link which is called the meaning associated with that sound of a language. If this association remains consistent through one's experience, then the sound triggers the perceived thing and conversely. Truth is in the perception of the thing (or its image as a substitute for it) and consistency of the association transfers the sense of truth from the thing to the accompanying sound. Thus, words gain their meaning and from such a connection we come to the conclusion that such a word *has* such a meaning.

Therefore, there are two universes of associated perceived realities in our mind. One universe is known directly through the dynamics of perception of the energy impacts and the other is made of the associations between them, not perceived themselves as things are (i.e. because of their intrinsic energy), but because they are capable of triggering in us those energies or their retained impacts.

What matters here, is that we are concerned with *two universes of perceptions* and with their dynamics within the self. Because from now on perceptions go in pairs — one triggering the other — the self can stress one or the other, as we all do when we use language.

Centuries, if not millennia, were needed to develop a system of sounds corresponding specifically to a multitude of awarenesses of perceptions. Because experiences differ and observation of the content of the experiences depends on individual minds, different proposals can be encountered in the different valleys of the earth. Not only the sounds proposed for one and the same thing (say, the sun, or a tree) differ from language to language but there are also differences in how perception of number, of quantity, of qualities, of temporality, of relative position, of activity, of intention, of actuality etc. are conveyed. Since awarenesses take time, since proposals may prove ineffectual, since lives are short and not all humans had to become proposers, we find all languages undergoing some historic processes, in which the influencing of one by another was not excluded.

A thorough comparative study of a number of languages shows that behind the many thousands of proposals available on earth today we can find some inescapable components that reveal the most primitive awarenesses without which the task at hand would have been impossible.

All languages presuppose the awareness of time simply because we have no means of producing simultaneously two sounds with our mouth. One must follow the other. All languages blend sound production with something else compatible with it, such as tone or stress, but no language can be produced that does more than place sounds one after the other, either merged together or separated from one another by silences.

Awareness of what can be done with one's throat with the various somatic components, voluntarily changeable, on the flow of air moving from the lungs to the open mouth, provides the registers for the many proposals at one of the ends of this production. Because such production is willed and because the human being producing it can also entertain another awareness, a principle is found at work in all languages and that is, that a perception of an alteration, a modification on, or a change in the field of perception is somehow made perceptible through the changes in the associated sound or sounds and conversely.

What we call roots, or stems of words, exist in all languages and vouch for the primitiveness of such an observation. It was found unnecessary to create a new word for every perception although this is a possibility, as happens on the pharmaceutical market when manufacturers want to keep them distinct for commercial reasons. But our linguist-ancestors — who met these problems for the first time — related to their awarenesses and found proposals in keeping with their imagination, their daring and their common sense. Since they could easily distinguish change in the order of sounds, change in the order of successive sets of sounds, or in additions or subtractions of sounds; since they could shift stresses, blend words, they resorted to such algebraic rules to guide their composition of sounds (to make words) which were distinguishable in the time dimension as well as in the awareness of the existence of specific sounds. Whenever proposals made by one individual could also be perceived by others and found practicable by them, acceptance by others became possible. However, the same challenge offered to other people in other valleys was met by a different solution.

Perceptible and practical are the two permanent features of all languages. The first is necessary to make sense, to connect with truth and reality; the second is necessary to lead to adoption by others. Practical in fact, only means that the equipment of the recipients of the proposal conforms to that of the proposer. (Practical is not here equivalent to universal although it may gain that meaning in the eyes of language teachers.)

Because all components of the modifiers in languages are perceptible to some people at least, all grammars are susceptible to expression in perceptible terms, i.e. through linguistic situations that bring to the fore the most intricate arrangements of sounds to display precisely the associated awarenesses.

Thus, in the realm of perception, our sensitivity tells us what we are perceiving. And since it can be an impact of energy initiated by a perceptible item or by a movement of energy within, we can associate two realms of perception and generate in ourselves a language.

We will best understand this in studying how babies learn to speak. We will manage to find in this process some things which our ancestors had to do to develop their language, although there is no suggestion here of a recapitulation by the individual of what the group has gone through.*

* * *

Babies have only themselves as guides in their apprenticeship of the language of the environment, however much the public believes that parents help in that apprenticeship. In fact, no one knows how to help a baby make sense of anything. They either do it on their own or it does not happen.

All babies who are not deaf, since they are left alone and to their own devices, will have many opportunities to make sounds and to listen to them. Becoming aware that they are equipped to make sounds by making them, babies have access to the workings of the flow of air as it moves from the lungs through

---

* In fact, a recapitulation is neither necessary nor feasible. Every baby finds in his environment a highly structured language in which innumerable distillations, filterings, developments have been at work, maybe for millennia. No requirement is made upon anyone to first produce the proto-language and all its alterations over centuries. In fact, all of these except the most recent ones are lost forever, thus making recapitulation impossible.

the throat into their mouth. Since all of the components of phonation are voluntary, every baby (including the deaf) can act upon the various variables involved and study them directly through the impact of air on sensitive surfaces and through the changes of muscle tone in selected muscles. From about the sixth week after birth, this study is done seriously, thoroughly, and in a concentrated manner. What a baby finds first is that the flow of air from the lungs through the larynx can be controlled and that the activities at the two ends can be coordinated. It then finds that the muscle tone of the lips is at its disposal, and he works on it for some time per se and then in coordination with the mastered skills. Simultaneously or separately, the walls of the mouth are worked on in terms of muscle tone. So every baby can survey in minute terms the muscular components which can be affected by the will and for whichever end it wills. Such inner direct knowledge is not only needed, it is an indispensable ingredient of that which will enable babies to direct their learning from now on. Hearing, (if it exists) is brought in quite early –

1 to serve as a feedback mechanism,

2 to supply a second set of criteria for a baby to know what it is doing and whether the energy output matches the project, and

3 after this, to provide a substitute system for what the baby has done consciously.

This substitution is accepted by the baby because it provides an immediate sounding board which has far less inertia than the other muscles and thus will produce a more flexible instrument to inform the self. Moreover, it will serve to produce the bridge between what one is able to do now within one's own system, and the impacts from the environment which are the preeminent ones.

For weeks or even months, babies give themselves a frame of reference for the immediate analysis, scrutiny of sounds received and for their translation into their own somatic equivalents. Without this referential, it is impossible to understand how babies manage to penetrate their verbal environment, and conquer it by their cracking of the spoken code.

Babies can do such work on their own because they are endowed with awareness and with a will to affect the muscle tone, and because they can —

1. note the results, and
2. go over processes as many times as is needed to produce complete certainty that they know what they are doing and to what avail, as well as know how to produce what they want.

All this gives babies the means to elaborate a very complex system of sound production which obeys determined orders and is monitored all the time for its "perfection" in the circumstances.

In particular, awareness of duration of individual sounds and clusters of sounds, of permutations of sounds (only requiring awareness of order in time) and of combinations of various sounds, awareness of intensity, of presence or absence of certain sounds, of the distribution of silences between sounds, all of which the baby is equipped to do.

Once babies concentrate on listening to sounds in the environment they can hear the multitude of sounds available: from the breeze in leaves of trees or the rattle of a toy in one's crib, of trucks passing by or the thunder. A baby will as easily know the distinctive attributes of voices other than its own. Going first to the most accessible properties present in the vehicles of speech (i.e. voices) babies recognize at once that the energy they receive through their ears from humans in the environment, is not random and they pay attention to objective features in it. As we noticed earlier, words are not the first component to be recognized. In fact, they are one of the last. Before words can be known, babies can reach all the non-verbal components which are second nature to all of us adults. We fail to recognize these components because familiarity wears out their capacity to strike us. Young babies are not yet made insensitive by familiarity and they experience the energy distributions of what they hear as true and real components.

In the same way as we are affected today by a musical melody we yield to, we have been affected by the equivalent of melody in speech when we were babies. Though every one of us uses his or her own voice for verbal expression, we all display ways of using our somatic functionings which tell that we speak our language as members of our group do. Accent and mode of producing utterances, more than grammar and vocabulary are what links each one of us to other members of definite groups. Since accent has a perceptible reality it can be grasped as soon as one embarks upon it or has decided to surrender to it. Hence, although each baby knows it has to use its own voice to express itself — and does this uniquely, all through life — it also knows that it is equipped to yield to the melodic components of the language in the environment and let this mold its speech. This melodic form of the language is an objective property of the energy distribution in each statement and is therefore directly perceivable. It is assimilated by the process of surrender to it and the retention of its impacts. So babies end up speaking like the people in their environment.

Energy distribution also concerns the affective component which is part of languages. This and all that goes with it, is made available to babies. In particular, what will later be labeled questions, interjections, doubts and affirmative or aggressive statements, will be transmitted as affective components and from them the comprehension of the oral language will follow. This oral comprehension is the backbone of all comprehension, including the comprehension of *reading*.

Babies have access to all these nonverbal components and because of this they can confirm to themselves their progress in their various apprenticeships. In particular, they find manageable the task of learning the most foreign of all the foreign languages, i.e. their first language.

Linguists have looked at languages in terms which make the intellectual feat of learning to speak seem either a miracle or an impossibility. Since almost all babies manage to learn to speak in the first twenty—four months of their life ex-utero, linguists must look at it again.

To acquire their first language, babies do only what they can, and that is to link the two universes of perceptions we talked about earlier: the perception of things and that of their concomitant sounds. In that, they do what our ancestors did. Having found how to command with precision their own sound production, babies will one day hear people around them utter what they themselves do utter. Here they find the illuminating link between their spontaneous sound utterances and that of others. Babies thus know that others do what they do and interpret what they hear in terms of utterances and manage to produce some sounds approximating more and more what others say. They can match in their auditory system (which includes the brain and mental experiences) what they hear and they retain and what they themselves can produce on their own initiative. They keep both within themselves and move from one to the other, until they produce, to their satisfaction, what they think others utter.

Thus, the empirical job of uttering what they hear coming from the environment and which they attribute to the people in it, continues as a major task for babies who may be only eight or nine months old. This is done independently of the acquisition of the melody, which has been accessible as a whole while these new items result essentially from new analyses. We are not yet concerned with meanings (in the sense of relating at the same time the perception of things to the perception of the concomitant sound or corresponding word in the language), but with what babies have to do to learn to speak the language of their environment. In our book *The Universe of Babies,* what we have just described was placed under the heading of *talking*.

Talking is the preparation every one of us gives oneself in order to ensure entry into that part of the language we can call verbal — perhaps only 20% of every language.

If we aim at a view of the apprenticeship of language that reflects the facts of learning in early childhood, it is imperative to see that the working of awareness provides both the sensitivity to what one is meeting and the suspended judgment which keeps one in contact with the task with the required involvement but *without expectation.* The phase of talking stretches over a number of months and is not only concerned with words (as linguists understand them) but also with all the other components of verbal expression i.e. also carried by the voice. Because hearing is also available (for the non-deaf person) the detailed study of what one's voice can do leads through hearing to a thorough concomitant study of the phenomena of sound. The dual system is coordinated in every possible way and becomes an integrated whole for most purposes, until a need to separate the components occurs.

The qualities of sound called pitch, intensity, continuity and coloratura, as well as the demands of each on its own spectrum, are given time and known thoroughly per se and in conjunction with one another. Only when the survey is sufficient to cover as many instances provided by the environment, will a baby allow itself to entertain concomitant attributes present in each situation. As mentioned earlier, it is when someone in the environment produces a sound that the baby already consciously produces, that the baby's recognition of the sound forms a link between what it does and now understands others are doing. This produces a shift of attention in the baby from the non-verbal elements to which it is connected, to the verbal universe. Thus a beginning of language as understood by the environment is now possible.

The complexity of that realm does not permit more than a cautious, sporadic attempt to come close to this content. The way babies choose to do this differs from one individual to another, but all of them have the good sense of attacking only one word at a time (in the beginning) in order to study the matching of what they utter to what they abstract from the voices of people around them. When they are satisfied that they know how to produce what they wish, using the arsenal accumulated in their talking, they integrate that new complex to all their other functionings and consequently they know that *they* know how to produce that sound in the way *they* heard it produced by others.

Once this is integrated, it is as much at one's disposal as all other functionings. Hence, for babies learning to speak, it is like any one of the other apprenticeships they engage in. It involves a thorough study with the whole self of the challenges involved without fussing and without asking for help, constantly testing progress and noting feedbacks from all sources. This tells them whether or not they are with the elements of the situation they need to be with in order to overcome the obstacles within and to be free to forge ahead.

At every moment, there is experimentation — conscious, deliberate experimentation — so as not to assimilate wrongly what they can apprehend well. They observe carefully what people in the environment do before passing to a subsequent stage of their apprenticeship.

Satisfied in conveying via single words, the meaning they have seen triggered in others, they will gather a number of isolated groups of words before attempting to use these in groupings as expert speakers do. They can notice that their progress is neither linear nor gradual, except in the sense that they learn words in time one after another and only begin to structure them in phrases and sentences when they can recognize these words within the chains or part of other people's speech and hold them as such. For instance, the particle that produces negations is used as an omnibus operator to apply to as many adjectives as are in their vocabulary; the particles that replace many nouns (and are known as pronouns) are soon discovered as more flexible than nouns, being far fewer and so more often used and more often met. The words that point at qualities easily perceived as co-present can be used together; the nouns that are consistent labels for familiar objects from which one receives and stores lots of impressions, seem to become the objects themselves through the images they trigger.

Indeed, for babies, words become triggers of images for a while before they are as easily triggered by the corresponding objects or their images. Then words merge in one's consciousness and become objects of the mind in the same way as images do and are indistinguishable from them. At that stage a child speaks like his elders even if his vocabulary remains restricted.

Experience of language and general experience are not to be considered as one and the same thing. Babies can have a very elaborate and profound experience of language, because it is their creation. They can use it very early with a very high degree of competence, and still, have little knowledge of the content of the universe. A child may be an excellent speaker and use his power of speech to augment his overall experience at a tender age (under two years). Speaking is a constellation of skills covering the demands of syntax, phonetics, semantics and so forth, that can be entertained per se and mastered per se, while other fields of experience are left untouched.

Because of this distinction between the extent of vocabulary and the mastery of the functioning of the language in oneself, we find very young children using language very competently to the amazement of adults, particularly, linguists and psychologists who know now abstract and how complicated languages are. Those children who perceive the hierarchy of language experience and the experience of the world and manage to become good speakers very early, tell us that what language asks for, in terms of awareness, is much less than is required by the perception of other components of the universe. Distance and causality for instance, are met much later, when children are more experienced.

This way of working, shown to us by children, will guide us in our presentation of what will help all children when they come to study the written version of their language. In particular, to spell out for us which powers of the mind are used in this field.

These powers include:

1 perception that there are specific entities (sounds) to be perceived and that it is the ear which is used for this;

2 that one of the two levels at which these entities operate is concerned with a set of arbitrary but consistent elements carried by voices which refer specifically to some perceptible items in the universe of relating;

3 that, at the other level, these items change in specific ways, dictated by specific alterations in the field of perception, in manners that can be perceived (such as distance, number or relativity);

4 that the special way the environment has chosen (regardless of the choice) to render its apprehension of the changes in the world *in* the verbal medium, is accessible to language learners provided only that it be perceptible and consistent;

5 since the number of items to be labeled, always exceeds by far the number of labels, language is experienced as a handy and economical way to attain aims which may be *within* one's reach or beyond it;

6 that the number of labels approximates the number of impressions once one knows how to affect the labels by applying prefixes and suffixes (to roots or stems) as the inventors of the language have proposed;

7 that the verbal part of language refers to intellectual components while the variations in the

vehicle refer to the affective and social components;

8 that one has to work first on expression, and when this is clear, communication has a chance to happen;

9 that the alterations upon words proposed by the ancestors (and which go to make the present state of the language as found in the environment) are a relatively small number and form an "algebra" akin to a dynamics accessible for use by the mind, in preference to retaining the vocabulary as if it were made of separate items;

10 that retention and recognition work for words in the way they work in all other fields to generate the content of a dynamic memory and they are applied here also;

11 that the fleeting nature of the temporal component of speech demands attention, simultaneous suspension of judgment till the end of a statement, and selective lighting of one's experience by the selection of the appropriate images that are triggered by the sounds as they are heard, and held if they make sense or rejected if they do not;

12 retention of the "meaning" as conveyed by a process which can be described as resulting in:

i. a more permanent energy change in oneself, and

ii. a withdrawal of the energy that was lent to the words during the process of listening.

These last two processes give to comprehension an objective reality in keeping with the function of words which are only substitutes for experience.

Certainly there are other lessons we can learn from our children while they are learning to speak. These will serve us in improving our teaching of language, reading, writing, spelling, comprehension, composition, because all these concern awarenesses involved in the functionings needed to master the spoken language.

We devote the next chapters of this book to this common sense use of the wealth of competence of children.

* * *

To sum up our findings so far, we can say that it is common sense to incorporate the gifts given freely by many, many children who are apprentices involved spontaneously in solving the problems of learning to speak. This is considered very hard by students of the field, yet the children solve it smoothly, elegantly, effortlessly, and thoroughly at a very early age.

Because most of us do solve those problems, it must be relatively easy, and we must see this solution in the light that children *do the right things* all the time. This new light of "doing the right things" is the one we selected and we shall use it in the following chapter. The closer we come to adopting ways of teaching that use the powers of the minds of children and let the challenge of the subject-matter guide us, the closer we shall be to finding how to allow learners to pay only the right price for learning to read, whatever this price is.

* * *

And this too, is common sense.

2 From Meanings to Words and From Words to Signs

With the observations and insights of the previous chapter at our disposal, we can now examine what our ancestors did when they decided to give a visible form to their speech. We can look at how their ideas may have affected the written language we want to present to our students.

In various places on earth, different proposals were made for the translation of speech into writing. Today, it is believed that "Romanization" or adoption of the Latin alphabet is the most economical answer to writing all languages. This may not be so, as we shall see later; other common sense solutions, preferable to this one for a number of reasons, may in fact exist.

Our ancestors, guided by common sense, noticed that speech was in time. They noticed that complete attention, and the ability to hold in one's mind the sequence of words, were necessary to capture the fleeting quality of speech. It was only when these conditions were met that one could think, "I heard you and can say what you said, but I have to say it again for you to know that I did." Our ancestors undertook to represent concretely those awarenesses carried by their voice and words. Before embarking on this task, they must have noticed that the main obstacle facing them was how to represent time.

The best representation of inner time is outer time. When we speak, we experience inner time, because, like walking or working, speaking involves an expenditure of energy which cannot be made all at once. Action always involves a time sequence, while sight and feeling, for instance, do not. When looking at a landscape we can perceive many items simultaneously; we can be hit at once by an emotion such as fear or anger. But we cannot act outside of time.

Immediate introspection tells us all this. We therefore adapt ourselves to the necessity of taking time to transmute what we experience into speech, what we hear into experiences. Awareness of time as the main component of these dynamics is the most primitive constituent of our living. Although inner and outer time differ, together they generate the experience of time about which scientists still know very little.

Our ancestors who got involved in producing a visible form for their speech, could not escape being aware of the importance of time and its demands. Hence, although it is the subtlest ingredient of speech, time must be given a prominent place in the solution to the problem of representing speech.

The art of drawing, practiced for thousands of years — as shown by cave decorations in Europe and art in the deserts of the American west — indicates that our ancestors must have faced very early the problem of time. These drawings prove that the observation of a reality grasped by humans could be transferred from sight to touch, from the eye to the hand. It took time for a draftsman to draw a buffalo on a wall; however, the finished drawing, when looked at as a whole, did not take time to be seen. Even if one scanned details, there was nothing in the drawing that forced one to look at a specific detail before another. Since all points are equally good as starting points in a visual analysis, it shows that sight does not impose a time sequence, as does action.

For the people who wanted to find a representation for what they said, the first thing that came to mind was *symbols*. A glance at Egyptian hieroglyphics or ancient Chinese characters makes this clear. The content of the mind is meanings. We experience words both as the triggers of meanings, and as being triggered by meanings. These meanings are associated with images, which accompany words. Images are of course, more easily rendered by a drawing which evokes them. Such drawings carry something of the object, but are not the object. Representations of words which evoke images are called symbols. The word *symbol* we shall reserve for a representation that keeps some perceptible relation to what it represents. Since letters and words no longer contain anything that is perceptibly recognizable, they are not symbols in this sense.

The ability of symbols to represent that which is perceptible was undoubtedly an advantage to our ancestors. However, this advantage of symbols soon becomes an unbearable servitude if the representation must reflect all that is perceptible. Many attributes of reality which can be perceived — such as distance, weight and speed — cannot be adequately represented. After many trials, our ancestors were probably forced to abandon the attempt to find enough symbols for the whole of perceptible reality, and to look for a more adequate solution.

This solution, found several times and taking several forms, was the substitution of arbitrary signs for real symbols. *Signs* are conventions recognized in advance as requiring agreement between the parties. Signs do not suggest anything by themselves. Anything could serve as a sign, since nothing is retained of the original perception. The use of arbitrary conventions in speech had already paved the way for the use of signs in writing. The oral language had established the use of arbitrary sounds to label experiences. The only requirement to make spoken words acceptable was, that they be consistent. Spoken words are arbitrary, but among the members of a community speaking a given language, they trigger images which are realities. The energy associated with spoken words endows them with a reality that leads the speakers to believe that what they are uttering is the reality itself to which the words refer.

The experience of the spoken language prepared our ancestors to shift from written symbols to signs. The Chinese have retained in their written characters some of the thinking of their ancestors. However, even they cannot claim today that their characters are symbols. Most of them are signs. Readers retain them by remembering them as associated mentally to an image such as that of an object. However, the image of an object is rarely found represented in the design of the character itself. Once the decision to abandon representation by symbols is reached, the problem becomes: which signs to adopt, and on what principles? Different groups in the various inhabited areas of the world reached different solutions. One solution has been to adopt the solution of those who have found one already. Such a solution, though it may have saved many generations years of trial and error, also created problems as we shall see.

In creating spoken languages, our ancestors had found that there were principles of economy which they used again and again. Examples of these are: giving several meanings to the same word; altering a root or stem by the addition of a prefix or suffix. Such alterations of a root are related to the perception of changes of meaning in a particular situation.

Our ancestors adopted similar principles of economy in creating written languages. They found they could make use of both in adopting solutions found by neighbors, and in creating a set of drawings that would serve as signs to represent spoken sounds.

Spoken English displays one of these principles of economy in a verbal algebra that generates words one from the other; examples of this algebra are offered by the sets *pat, tap, apt,* and *top, pot, opt.* The words within each group are permutations of three sounds; when going from one set to the other, words are formed by substitution. *Reversal,* of which two examples are found in the sets above, is one of the most common permutations. There are numerous such pairs of reversals in the spoken language. The following are illustrations: *less* and *sell, sick* and *kiss, map* and *pam, funny* and *enough*. We invite readers to find examples of their own. When we look at these words as they are written, we find that much more than an alphabet is required to transliterate sounded words. These requirements are to be found in the chapter on spelling (Chapter 6). Nevertheless, we can say here that we are helped considerably in the study of language if we keep in mind that reading and writing owe a great deal to speaking. Many problems that we consider to be reading problems result from an insufficient analysis of their equivalents in the spoken language.

Our ancestors were aware that the principle of economy was made manifest in a spoken language through what we called an algebra. They knew, too, that this algebra operated independently of the meanings of the words. They therefore used it in the transcription of a spoken language into writing; ideogrammatic scripts are the exception.

Our ancestors could not have mastered the challenges of language transcription without two awarenesses:

1 that they must make time visible,

and

2 that they must economize.

We have already discussed the second problem; let us examine the first along with its solution. Space is a reality that our ancestors could become familiar with just as we can. Therefore, they must have discovered, at some time, that *only the straight line* (and the spaces homeomorphic to it) can be used to render the properties of time. Time lived and time remembered have the structure of successive instants related by the awareness that is rendered in language by the words "before" and "after." A Newtonian "flux" generates durations from instants. Durations either precede or follow or overlap each other. This creates, in the structure of time, an order and a measure very similar to that of points and segments on a straight line. These awarenesses were accessible to our ancestors, as they are to us. So, we must not marvel at the fact that *all* inventors of writing selected to arrange in linear order the signs chosen to trigger the sounds of their diverse languages.

The use of the straight line to represent time is a fundamental convention in writing. A corollary to this convention is *direction*. Time lived is irreversible, and only one of the two possible directions on the straight line can represent the continuing flow of time lived. Speakers of various languages have either selected to write on horizontal lines from right to left (for most languages) or from left to right (the other languages) or from top to bottom on vertical lines (Chinese and Japanese).

People today generally accept the written form given to their languages by their ancestors, although there are a few exceptions. Chinese and Japanese today are written horizontally as well as vertically, generally from left to right. The convention of aligning written characters on a straight line, introduced by our ancestors, now appears natural to us. This is because we, like our ancestors, can be sensitive to the fact that, in transcribing sound into sign, the straight line lends itself particularly well to the representation of time. A corollary to this convention is that, if the spoken statement is of greater duration than can be rendered by a single printed line, we extend it over a number of parallel lines. These may be ordered from top to bottom, from left to right, or from right to left.

The arrangements of lines on paper found in all books may be called *necessary conventions*. They are imposed by the nature of the awarenesses of time and space, and of the use of the second to represent the first. This is why, though written languages may otherwise differ completely, these conventions are found in all of them.

Past generations in a variety of civilizations and cultures made different suggestions for written languages. Knowing about these various suggestions may help us to establish a hierarchy of things to present to beginners who must master the conventions of writing for their language.

The following examples will give an idea of the variety of solutions proposed by various civilizations:

1 In many languages, signs are placed on top of the lines. However, in languages derived from Sanskrit, signs hang from the lines.

2 Words may be separated one from the other, as they are in this text. In Thai, however, a whole sentence is written as one contiguous string. In Sanskrit and German or Lakotan, some of this convention still operates; in all other languages

except Chinese and Japanese, its operation is reflected by the use of hyphenation.

3 In many languages there are special signs which represent not words but aspects of the act of reading aloud. For instance, exclamation points and question marks indicate qualities of the voice; commas and periods indicate pauses. In some languages these marks do not exist, and are not felt to be necessary.

4 In many languages there are two typefaces for the same letters — capitals and lower case.

These conventions differ in kind from those which our study of time led us to term "necessary." Since people can write and read without them, they are surely not necessary. They may be helpful and useful for some functions; they may make people into better readers and writers. Nevertheless, they are not at the basis of the hierarchy of the "musts" which will make people into readers and writers. In a way these conventions are a luxury and can be offered to students when they can afford them. This is a common sense position.

Looking at a number of written languages, we see that each of them makes a number of demands on students. We see also that once native speakers have mastered the demands of the written language, it provides them with the means of expressing most of the content of their consciousness. In examining what readers and writers of a language have done to meet the demands of the written language, we become aware that some of these demands are much better met after others. It is therefore, not wise to ask our students to consider them simultaneously. As teachers, we would be wise to define the hierarchy of problems we want to present to our pupils. It makes sense to concentrate first on the necessary conventions. When these have become second nature to our pupils, we may introduce the non-necessary conventions chosen by the culture. It is possible to introduce these one by one through activities that make students aware of the basis for choosing these conventions, and then give them sufficient practice for integrating each new convention to the overall activity of reading and writing.

It is now possible to discuss the complex convention of choosing particular signs to trigger certain sounds. Alphabetic languages use a convention in the formation of words that may be described theoretically as "a set of *letters* placed contiguously to indicate which sounds are to be uttered and in which order." We said "theoretically" because in actuality written languages have allowed ambiguities to become part of them. Hence, in many languages letters do not indicate which sounds are to be produced. Sometimes groups of letters must be taken as the signs which trigger single sounds, and it is necessary to know what sound will be triggered by that sign in different situations. These ambiguities complicate the straightforward method of decoding as the basis for reading, and create the problem of spelling in writing.

If an alphabetical language exists in which each sign is assigned only one sound, and each sound is represented by one sign only, we may call it phonetic. Although a number of languages come close to being phonetic, as far as I know there are none that are truly phonetic. Many sounds are altered by contiguity with other sounds. Strictly speaking, a truly phonetic language would have to provide a separate sign for each of these sounds; English would then need thousands of signs. This requirement of purists seems impractical; since most of us have managed to compensate for some of the gaps left by the 26 — letter alphabet, we shall avoid joining their ranks.

Different types of alphabets have been chosen by different peoples in different parts of the world. Only three of the vowels of Arabic have a sign of their own; the others are not written. Therefore, reading a word in Arabic (or Hebrew) requires some knowledge of the language apart from what is given by the printed word. Amharic and Japanese have alphabets that refer to vowels and syllables. English uses vowels, diphthongs, consonants and syllables. Although the appearances tell us that English is alphabetic, it certainly is not phonetic.

English is not a phonetic language; however, this fact has nothing to do with the demands of reading. Reading in a language that is phonetic is a straightforward activity for native speakers, as soon as they have mastered the basic sound-sign conventions. In the case of a non-phonetic language, such as English, the challenge is very complex. Many reading teachers are imbued with the prejudice that learning the alphabet has something to do with reading. If we are to bring some common sense into the teaching of reading, this may be one of the prejudices that needs to be eradicated.

Our ancestors made the mistake of choosing the Latin alphabet to represent the sounds of English. A number of people have proposed reforms (cf. Chapter 6; *On Spelling);* but none of these has been generally accepted. Perhaps the answer is to attempt to live with this mistake and to consider the conventions of the alphabet as a historical fact. They will only be binding in that the final product of one's writing must look like what other writers put down in their texts. To write in English will therefore be to use words that display the "orthography" acceptable to those who are the arbiters in that field.

In this book we do not suggest a reform, but only techniques which are valid for reading in any language, alphabetic or not, phonetic or not. Concentrating here on the case of English which is an alphabetic nonphonetic language, we shall develop our approach as though there were only such languages in the world. Transfer of the approach to other languages is possible, and has been worked out for between 20 and 30 languages.

We know now that we are asking those who wish to become readers to meet the apparently simple challenge of making sounds which correspond to strings of signs ordered on a line in a certain way. If we reflect, however, we also see that we cannot just ask them to do this without some preparation. They may be perfectly able to master the demands of the challenge, but still not learn to read or write because the hierarchy of the activities has not been made clear to them. In the rest of this book, we are guided by the hierarchy of activities we found necessary for reading.

Most of us, as small children, learned to speak. We must have used ourselves in such a way that we knew all the time that we were doing the right thing to acquire the spoken language. In studying the hierarchy of activities necessary for reading, we must therefore begin by asking ourselves two questions: what is the act of reading, and how can we use ourselves in learning to read as we did in learning to speak — that is, in a way that we know we are doing the right thing all the time. What we now need to acquire is what distinguishes the written language from the spoken one.

In order to understand the act of reading, and acquire all the skills for writing, we need to know that for most readers each word tells what needs to be said for it. The written word holds the clues that tell us to utter *this* word and no other. However, this knowledge does not suffice to make one into a reader. Writing transcribes only a part of what each speaking voice carries. Therefore, in the activity of uttering words on the printed page, the reader must make adjustments to insert the missing elements. Reading, in the beginning, involves restoring voice to words on the printed page, so that in uttering them one hears again the spoken language with which one is familiar. Later one may modulate this capacity to restore the sounds of the spoken language to written signs, so that one masters other aspects of reading such as reading silently, reading faster and faster, and even reading only a few words in each statement and inferring the total meaning from these.

In this chapter, we are concerned with the beginnings; we therefore don't have to ask our students to develop any of the skills that can be developed later. Working on the fundamentals provides students with enough challenges so that they will not mind postponing, for a few weeks or months, other aims which are desirable, but which are dependent on the basic masteries.

The fundamental discipline in reading and writing has been acquired when one says only what each printed word requires, and when one has disciplined oneself so that one can accurately write strings of sounds dictated. After acquiring the fundamental discipline, each learner has to find out that:

1. Running words together, or *phrasing*, is a component of reading. Equal spaces are left between words on the printed page, but this is a non-necessary convention, and is only a convenience for typesetters. In restoring a voice to printed words, we run them together; phrasing goes counter to the convention of spacing between words. Phrasing is in fact an adjustment of the voice that either gives the spaces between printed words their value of silences between groups of words, or makes us treat them as though they were nonexistent.

2. Words of more than one syllable display another energy component called *stress* or *emphasis* that affects meaning. Sensitivity to this component will help in lending a text the character of spoken discourse, and even more so if intonation also is taken into account.

3. *Intonation* is seen as an attribute of the spoken language that carries a good part of the meaning because it is energy and forces awarenesses that the uniform printed words do not elicit from beginners.

A printed text originates in spoken statements, affected by both the author's experience and the traditions of the language. Therefore, the insertion of the melody of the spoken language into the utterances made while reading, produces a required ingredient for the understanding of the text. Sometimes comprehension may be immediate and total, without much attention to the melody. But often the melody betrays a necessary mood or intuition beyond the words. *Melody* is therefore needed if one wants to achieve comprehension. In the case of silent reading, its use will have to become virtual.

We are fully conscious that the transfer from mastered spoken language to the apprenticeship in reading is the job of teaching. Our approach "Words in Color" therefore provides techniques and materials that offer students activities which generate that transfer.

We use color to trigger the various sounds in order to avoid the automatic mechanism of repeating the sounds someone else has said, since we know that the sounds are already part of the student. It is an obvious convention; the relating of a particular color to a particular sound is absolutely arbitrary, but it remains consistent throughout. Color also assists with the task of mastering the capricious spellings of English by associating these to the proper sound. The black background has been deliberately chosen to allow the colored signs to stand out in relief, since it is these which trigger the desired sounds. The use of charts makes it possible to display on a wall a collection of words which will be available to students as long as they are in front of them, and which they can interpret on their own. We use the pointer to join words on the charts in order to generate a vast number of statements whose construction is at the appropriate level for the students. They can also produce statements of their own. They can show their work to classmates who can judge whether their own criteria are satisfied or not. They can collectively generate a sequence of statements that sound like a story.

Thus, the charts relate the shapes of some words to their sounds by means of the colors. The use of the pointer provides the students with the reality of the time sequence. The speed with which words are joined by the pointer tells students which words need to be run together in order to generate the phrasings that go to make the melodies in each sentence.

Besides these word charts which are displayed on the wall, there are four primer books called R_0, R_1, R_2 and R_3. These books take care of the hierarchy of the activities of reading which will be studied in detail in the next four chapters. R_0 takes care of the discipline of reading, R_1 the confidence of reading well, R_2 the survey of all the sounds of English, and R_3 spelling. These form the subject matter of Chapters 3, 4, 5 and 6 respectively. There are other chapters in this book, but they are concerned with further "*R*"s that represent further levels of mastery.

The following diagram sums up the evolution of a learner who is able to speak what he feels and thinks, and then adds to this power the ability to transmute all that he can say into written language.

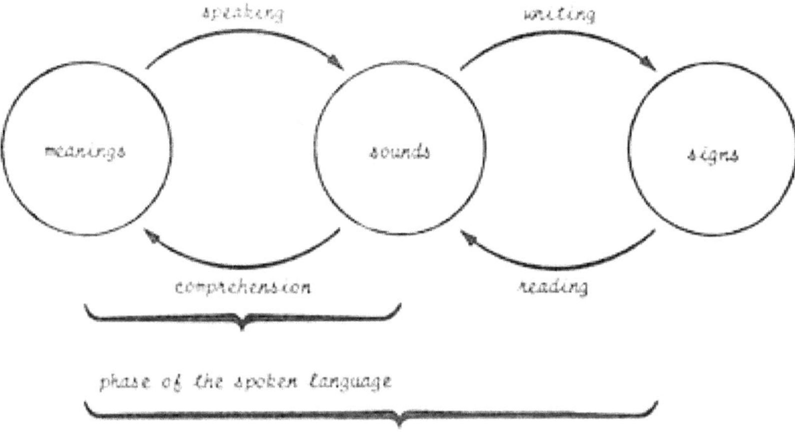

This schema is to be understood dynamically. When *meanings* expand for whatever reason, the spoken language of *sounds* can follow suit. If the techniques for putting down *sounds* exist, *signs* follow suit, expanding the reading and writing experience of the learners. In reverse, once reading as a technique is available *signs* trigger *sounds* of the spoken language, and these spoken words generate comprehension because they are already linked with the way in which the learner interprets his experience.

Part II

From “R_0” to “R_3”

3 The Act of Reading and the Discipline of Reading

The Act of Reading

Because so many of us learn to read during our school years, the act of reading, in which most of us involve ourselves, is not a popular subject of study. In this chapter, we shall consider a number of aspects of this act from which we shall find some guidance in our work on teaching reading.

The act of reading is different from reading, in that we are not concerned with getting at the content of a text we read, but are concerned with the reader and what he or she does in order to relate to the written words. How meaning gets produced will be studied in many places in this book.

For people with sight the act of reading involves the eyes; for blind people, the fingertips.

Since the number of sighted people is much larger than that of the blind, we shall concentrate first on the role of the eyes. If our findings are correct, we may discover that a simple transformation will help us understand how they apply to the blind.

Like me, most readers know that they can shut one eye and still read as easily as if two were open. Since one eye is as capable as two to do all the jobs we can think of, does one eye do one thing during the time we spend reading, while the other does something else?

In fact, the act of reading can be better understood if we look at those individual components of reading which compose the overall act of reading.

* * *

When he was two and not yet speaking, my son sat in front of me turning the pages of a book he was holding on his lap. Clearly communicating with me, he looked at me with a smile as if to say: "If what you are doing is the same as what I see you doing, turning the pages of a book, I can do it too. I can do that thing which is one of the activities involved in the act of reading."

Until then, I had not counted this turning of pages as an individual component in my activity as a reader, but a two-year old, who could not perceive the rest of the act, had access to it and made it plain.

Although it may seem laughable to some, I shall begin with the two most obvious components of the act of reading:

1 getting hold of a text to look at, and

2 when that text is a multi-page one, turning the pages on certain signals, e.g., coming to the end of the page.

After this I count as another component, opening the book in a definite way: from the left cover for some languages, from the right for others.

Another is looking at a page to allow something on it to reach us. If it is a picture, we relate to it in certain ways; if it is a set of written sentences, in others.

Pictures, like landscapes, affect us simultaneously from many spots and we can let them all have equal status on our mind. If color is involved, we also perceive the various photons reflected from the page as a number of colors. But we can also use another power of our mind and focus on a detail, or while focusing, scan the picture. In this dialogue, we find that the impact can remain with us and that we can re-evoke some of it by closing our eyes and ordering our image-producing mechanisms to provide us with this image, and no other.

In this exercise, we discover that one way of retaining visual material is to look at it, and if it makes sense to us, we find the following: what is retained is akin to the source, it is unequally vivid, some of its details have more significance than others, some need to be looked at again to yield their content, and it is impossible to verbalize exactly what one sees.

If we attempt this last transmutation, the statement we end up with is adequate only when we are prepared to say more and more words, as we feel the discrepancy between our visual impression and the impression our words create.

When we look at a page on which only words appear, there are simultaneous impacts from all places on the page on our retina. We can become aware of the form of any one of the words by focusing on it. This makes seeing words and seeing pictures the same kind of activity. If we look at a script we do not know, the impression is precisely the one described above, and if we know how to draw, we can reproduce the detail of that "landscape" as if it had been taken from a picture page.

We therefore have the challenge of understanding what we do mentally when we move from being a sighted person, who looks at print, to being a person who reads it.

The qualifier "mentally" is required here, for we do not do anything to our eyes optically since we still can see the page. The act of reading is essentially a discipline of the mind. We use our eyes, but we "stress and ignore" differently in the two activities described above.

To become a reader one needs to acquire what all of us readers already own. To teach beginning readers, we need to know what we acquired, which is now so much second nature that we find it difficult to reach. Because it has not been reached introspectively in a sufficiently precise and usable manner, there are many people who have not been able to learn on their own and some who have not been able to be taught. In as well-administered and financed a community as the United States, all of the experiments in the act of reading have not brought enough light to conclude: "If one does certain things with oneself, no one, who can see and has learned to speak, will fail to learn to read."

Because of this gap in these studies, the fault is placed on the students or on the complexities of the language. Teachers work with those who somehow manage to make sense of the act of reading, and so are free to embark on it spontaneously whenever they become interested. Little attention is given to understanding the few simple things that will help to make sense of it to any learner.

* * *

As teachers of reading, we have accepted too easily the conclusions of specialists in other areas: the physiologists and the psychologists of perception. The accumulated research is impressive, but its impact has been almost negligible.

Instead of relying on laboratory findings, we can use common sense. We note that since speech is in time, the first awareness to acquire is that: the spatial representation of time is the straight line. We must learn to hold our sight on the straight line and follow this by focusing on one word at a time, penetrating its structure to find a sequence of signs which trigger a sequence of sounds which we reproduce to form spoken words. Because time is irreversible, with any word (however small) the progression we follow within the word must begin either on the left or the right, according to which convention has been chosen by the language we are reading. If this is not learned with certainty, confusions may result.

We have learned from those who have studied visual perception that some weeks after birth, we manage to coordinate the two images obtained by our two eyes on our retina. *We say* we do this in our "mind" or in our "brain" according to the type of investigator *we consider ourselves to be.* We learn to render parallel the axes of our two eyes, except if we suffer from strabismus. Since most of us, most of the time, see one object where we think there is only one, we conclude that two-eyed vision is simply a coordination of the two images. In fact, it is much more complex than that. For instance, it was said that we use the two eyes to form stereoscopic images. Observation of people born with one eye, when they learn to see indicates that they can make such images in three dimensions with one eye alone and can manipulate dangerous tools as skillfully as people with vision in both eyes. People with binary vision when trying to catch one of their hairs while looking at themselves in a mirror, know that their three-dimensional perception is a mental construct rather than a cerebral coordination working correctly by itself.

Since learning to read is not a requirement from nature but a social conditioning, the two eyes may have two blended functions. One is used to focus on a word and to scrutinize it, while the other eye is doing something else. To know what the other eye is doing, we need to reflect and design experiments to that effect.

Most of us have a "dominant eye," that is, an eye we use more consciously than the other to perform the looking we produce through our will. We delegate to it the job of focusing and of retention. We select to use this eye in learning to read and thus we can say, if the dominant eye is the right eye, that the job of the left eye may be to confirm whether the reading was correct or not, when we read from left to right. If we are "left dominant," the left eye does the focusing and the right one can move ahead either confusing the issue by feeding in information that the reader does not know how to process, or instead, preparing the reader to move on faster because of that information.

People who can read two languages with which they are equally familiar, but which use opposite directions in horizontal writing, may, and do find that their reading is not as easy and swift in one language as in the other because their eyes may not change dominance when they change languages. Such individuals occasionally discover the reason when they become aware of this discrepancy. Some circumstances, such as an eye operation or a sudden deterioration of one's vision *in one eye as compared to the other,* can also teach us clinically that a transfer of dominance is possible. Such circumstances can lead to some discoveries about what we did for years with two eyes and what we do now. This can serve as a basis for more searching investigations that would help us to treat non-readers without thinking of them as dyslexic or brain damaged. For instance, it may be sufficient to place an eye band on one of a student's eyes to free him or her from the confusion mentioned above or to let that student recognize that in this case using only one eye is more helpful for reading than using both. Since the *act* of reading is basic, we must give our attention to such matters every time we meet someone with reading difficulties.

The Discipline of Reading

Besides the possibility that having two eyes at work is not always better than one, we have to recognize the importance of the actual discipline of reading that we define as, "saying only that which a written word requests us to say."

We can say that we have managed to acquire this discipline when we —

1 stop guessing at the word,

2 look attentively at a word, and

3 sound it in the way the conventions of the language demand.

When we do this all the time, we can say that we are using the discipline of reading as it is related to the conscious and deliberate enunciation of words in the way those who know how to read would do.

Whether comprehension takes place or not is not our problem here yet. The discipline of reading has been separated from the rest of the activities of reading so that beginning readers enter into it in a way that will remove the obstacles which these students encounter when faced with reading a text.

* * *

We gave a name to this set of challenges; "R_o" and we teach that kind of reading in all alphabetic languages for which we have prepared materials.

In the case of English, R_o is also the title of a booklet that is put in the hands of beginners. Although not immediately understandable because of its strangeness, the booklet has features that make it one of the pillars of our approach to universal literacy.

If the reader has access to a copy of the booklet R_o, much of what follows will be much easier to grasp.

To begin with, we note that quite a number of conventions can be lumped together and made evident to students without using any words, when we accept to work on an artificial language made up of only one sound and one sign. There are of course a number of choices. The one we selected in this R_o is the sign *a* with which we associate the sound given in the English word *at*.

We demonstrate, in the case of this language of one-sign one-sound, what can obviously be repeated with another example, should readers choose to do so. If teachers examine what is being said here in order to find out why we suggest this beginning instead of any other, they may get the best possible entry into our approach. Moreover, it pays when teaching beginners to give as much attention as possible to this acquisition of discipline, so widely neglected, in general.

The letter *a* is drawn on the chalkboard using a piece of beige chalk, if available. The teacher while touching it with a pointer says the sound selected for it (as found in *at, am, an,* etc.), and immediately after that uses the pointer to tap twice under the sign *a* to elicit "*a*" "*a*" from the students; and then taps three times to elicit "*a*" "*a*" "*a*."

Once this is secured, we can play an elaborate game acting upon the time between tappings. For example, if what is said is transcribed by placing signs on a chalkboard, then signs placed close to each other will be uttered rapidly one after the other, while those separated by a blank will be separated by a short silence, and the transcription looks something like this:

—*a* *aa* *aaa* or — *aa* *a* *aaa*
or — *aaa* *a* *aa* etc.

Page 5 and 6* of the "book" R_o provide examples of the "sentences" which can be:

1 dictated to the student who could then tap it out on the chalkboard in the manner used by the teacher;

2 tapped by the teacher, uttered by one or more students;

---

* Editor's Note: Page numbers have been updated to refer to 2010 edition Reading Primers.

3 tapped by the teacher and written by a student on the chalkboard for all to see and comment upon;

4 tapped by the teacher, then uttered and written down by all students, with possibly one of them doing it on the chalkboard;

5 tapped by a student, uttered by him or her and written down on the chalkboard by that student or another;

6 tapped by a student and put down on paper by all without any utterance. Then, exchanging their written work, one student reads what is written and this is commented upon by everyone. If incorrect, it is corrected by someone to everyone's approval, including the teacher's. If correct, work continues in a like manner, "sentences" being read by the same student or by another.

All these activities are meant to ensure awareness of mastery of the components of the act of reading in that language. How long these exercises will last is a function of who is attending the class as well as who the teacher is. It may be a half hour operation or more, but if done well, it will not require *more* than one hour with a group of beginners comparable to those found in any kindergarten or first grade class.

The variation in size of the letter *a* as presented on page 5 of R_o, serves to convey that form, not size, is what matters in this activity.

* * *

Looking at the successive pages of *Ro*, it is clear that the same work could be done with any of the five vowels selected. Since learning is cumulative, if a thorough study of one of the vowels has been done, the time required for each of the successive vowels will be shorter and the level of the challenge can be raised.

And since there is more than one sign introduced (with its sound) as soon as two or more have been introduced, the complexity allowed by using more than one of the signs in forming words enables students to test their ability to shift from the sounding of one sign to the sounding of another when this is indicated by their order in the "words" and "sentences" which appear in the booklet. Since alternation and repetition are available the possibilities are infinite.

This too, can be seen in *Ro*. The important contribution of common sense here is that it makes us distinguish *awareness from facility*. It makes us note that some awareness may be transferable and, therefore, does not need for the same facility the thorough grounding that was given in the beginning. Common sense tells us that if pages 5 and 6 required one hour to achieve mastery, then pages 9 and 10 will require less time, 13 and 14 still less, and so on until the "book" is "read" in the first school week by this kind of exercise.

It is important to note that our only aim is to give our students the discipline of reading and to ensure that when they look at a group of letters aligned on paper, they can utter exactly what the teacher would, showing awareness of the act of reading with the five conventions* clearly observed.

The "meaning" in all this *is* the awareness of the conventions and there is no doubt that if teachers do what is described above, evidence of it will be constantly forthcoming.

Thus, it is possible to provide students with the discipline of reading so that they do not hold any confusion in their mind about what it is to read a language that does not yet trigger the meaning which experience in society permits. This kind of experience we shall encounter very soon and it will resemble the one basic for the spontaneous speech of the students.

Because in "R_o" we separate the act of reading from all the other demands that come from contact with a text, we can expect that all of the problems, which result from a lack of mastery of the discipline, will now vanish and that fewer non-readers will be found to be "brain damaged" or "dyslexic" than is the case today.

It is important to note that *the reality of time,* which gives a meaning to the existence of a definite sequence in the sounds uttered, is now integrated and that the convention of left to right reading, adopted by English, loses its arbitrariness and very soon becomes second nature, because it reflects a tangible reality: order.

---

* These five conventions are: 1) writing on lines, 2) from left to right, 3) from top to bottom, 4) leaving space between words, and 5) using signs to trigger sounds.

It is also important to note that the convention of a-sign-for-a-sound becomes a trigger now. Since this will remain throughout the apprenticeship of reading, it too will lose its arbitrariness and gain the reality of the triggers which are made part of perception.

Nothing of what we did in instilling the discipline of reading will have to be unlearned. If one adopts another set of conventions when studying a second language, for example, Arabic or Chinese, then what one transfers is an awareness that some signs were adopted arbitrarily for some sounds, but also the awareness that a direction is needed to display the irreversibility of time.

In what we said about "R_o," we only mentioned the use of color once, when we said that we gave the color beige to *a* for that sound. In fact, we use colored chalks when writing on the chalkboard as an additional indicator, when they are first introduced, to suggest that sound is to accompany the signs and that difference in color alerts us to a difference in sound.

We gave a pale yellow tint to *u* which will link it from now on to the first sound in *up* and *us*; a red rose tint to *i* to request the first sound in *it* or *is;* a pale blue tint to *e* to suggest the middle sound in *set* or *pet;* and white to *o* to suggest the middle sound in *pot* or *top*.

The use of color allows us to introduce two games which can serve students well.

<u>Game 1:</u> We have a sound-color chart made up of colored rectangles, the first five of which are colored in the five tints mentioned above. By putting it up on the wall and by pointing to the appropriate rectangles in a certain order, teachers can elicit from their students all the "words" contained in R_o.

A game, such as this, can be followed by an exercise in transcription. The students, using letters put down that which they know are associated with the rectangles pointed to: for example, *"iiaeaa."*

This game can be played long enough to familiarize the students with the color-sound relationship of the chart we call *Fidel*[*] and to prepare the ground for what will come later. If students know how to transliterate the pointing, this game can be stopped at once.

<u>Game 2:</u> Taking five pieces of colored chalk, the teacher can produce trains of colored rectangles on the chalkboard to indicate a "word" or a "sentence" by the color convention adopted. For instance:

beige beige white blue red rose

would indicate a "word" *aaoie* which can be made into several different "sentences" by varying the spacing in between the rectangles. For example:

---

[*] An Ethiopian word.

- aa oe i	*- a aoe i*	*- a ao ei*
- aao ei	*- aa oei*	*etc. . . .*

These two games, if kept at a level of difficulty just manageable by the students and not made to last too long, will in most cases be welcome and serve some worthwhile purpose.

Of course, these games are not necessary to ensure good reading. Yet they may prove very helpful in a number of cases. We recommend their use in these situations so that such students will avoid having to struggle later on.

* * *

The act of reading has led us to promote the discipline of reading. Since we can find that they are present in reading a text and in writing a text at any level of difficulty, this justifies our having taken the time they require to be mastered.

"R_o" is one of the features of our approach that is not acceptable at once by reading teachers. Until the concept of the discipline of reading is part of one's introduction to the challenge of reading to beginners, force of habit will suggest that "meaning," in the social sense, is preferred and "R_o" will be dismissed.

Common sense asks that what is necessary in developing a mastery be given. And "R_o" is certainly that. Many young children who are said to confuse words like *was* and *saw* can now be made aware that it is not just the similarity of the overall image or just the particular letters included that determines what the word is, but clearly they must include another dynamic — that is, the order (and direction) on the line which determines the order of the sounds in time. More often than not, such a simple awareness makes one recast an existing faulty habit and develop the correct one. In remedial cases, the students, whatever their age, welcome the illumination that "R_o" brings to their mind. They often express surprise that such a primitive set of exercises as are given in "R_o" can make them look at words as temporal sequences rather than as drawings whose aspects are seen simultaneously.

In the case of teaching people to read English, this may be the place to say a word about the absurdity of teaching the alphabet and expecting learners to be helped by it. The teaching of the alphabet for reading does, on the whole, the opposite of what "R_o" attempts to do: it deliberately creates a confusion that is unnecessary.

Letters, once written, gain a reality one may want to label. Letters treated as objects may require names like all other objects about which we speak. *These names are only justified in that context.* However, in the context of learning to read, "pea aye tea" must be thoroughly transformed before one can produce the expected "pat." The *transformations* required are simply ignored by most teachers even though they are the basis of the act of reading English in the alphabetic or phonic approach.

We already observed in a previous chapter that the ambiguities of written English are such that one letter, for example, *a,* may be used to trigger eleven sounds, and that one sound, the schwa ə is represented by twenty-four spellings. So we teach a lie when we tell beginners that *a* is "*a*" as in *"late"* for it can be any of the other ten as well.

That would not be too bad, if the alphabet in English helped in making words sound as they do. However, this is clearly not the case. A number of adults who went to school and failed to learn to read, when examined, proved to have been totally unable to overcome this single element of nonsense represented by the discipline of "spelling" a word in order to utter its conventional sound. Because they could not make sense of this way of working, many gave up and never benefited from their schooling in the field of language arts. In order to remedy their cases, one had to start again with the true discipline of reading and abandon altogether, any reference to the names of the letters, however painful the struggle.

When reading teachers confront the complete Fidel (cf. next Chapter and Chapter 6) and are asked to point to a word whose spelling is second nature to them, they find it difficult in the beginning to break through the barrier of the names of the letters and to reach the clusters of letters used in English to render single sounds and thus functioning as a single sign, like *th* which remains in their awareness *"t"* and *"h"* or like *igh* which remains *"i"* *"g"* and *"h"* etc.

When we avoid reference to the letters, as is possible through the techniques and materials of *Words in Color,* we prepare learners to become good, fluent and responsible readers.

4 Making Sense of Written Statements

Soon after we find that our students have the discipline of reading at their disposal, we can use it to provide them with an entry into the awareness that *this* discipline can produce sounds "strangely similar" to their own spoken language.

When the letters called "consonants" were given that label by someone in the past, the label was selected to convey that such signs were perceived as not sounding on their own. They needed to be blended with a vowel in order to be sounded. Hence they were named con-sonant or those that sound-with. Therefore, it is not correct to say that vowels and consonants are the bricks of speech. Instead we should say that vowels and *syllables* serve this function. The word "syllable" here is used solely to indicate a pair made of one consonant with one vowel, since a vowel is needed for sounding the consonant.

Referring to a number of names for letters of the alphabet, we find that they are indeed syllables: for example *"bee"* for *b,* and *"tea"* for *t*. Some teachers, preferring not to "name" but rather to "sound" the consonant, believe that they have dropped any vowel sound and do not hear that they are sounding a "schwa" with the consonant when they say "bə." In fact a vowel is needed for hearing most consonants, and common sense suggests that we do not distort facts to make them agree with our beliefs.

We shall adopt the division of sounds into vowels and syllables but accept to present our students with two sets we shall call vowels and consonants respectively — but using a new discipline in our teaching to ensure the mastery of the next stage in reading.

On both Fidel charts (the one of colored rectangles or the one with colored columns of signs*), we have given the top part to vowels and the bottom part to consonants. Yet, in using it, we *never* sound a consonant by itself, but wait until the pointer has touched both a consonant and a vowel and then sound both blended together as a syllable. The teacher can use an array (like that found in Book R_1 on the top of page 28) written on the chalkboard with colored chalks:

a u i e o

p

In order to introduce our beginner students to the rules of the new game, we concern ourselves with one consonant which we call the "brown one" whose shape is *p*; but it has no sound of its

---

* cf. Appendix A

own. If with the pointer we join one of the five known vowels to the brown one, either preceding it or following it, we can then sound *"ap"* or *"pa,"* *"up"* or *"pu,"* *"ip"* or *"pi,"* *"ep"* or *"pe,"* *"op"* or *"po,"* giving to *p* its conventional general value in English.

To elicit these sounds from beginners it may be sufficient to give them one of the syllables orally and ask student to "reverse it," as we reverse the movement of the pointer. Thus, they utter the same two sounds in reverse order. When they write either syllable, they respect the time sequence by writing first what they utter first.

Although we did not mention it in the previous chapter, in "R_0" we have already had many opportunities to practice reversing sequences of sounds. In case teachers do not believe their students will be able to reverse syllables, we suggest they introduce reversal as a mental operation, as well as label it *"reversal"* when two vowels are blended: *ai* and *ia* are reversals one of the other.

Reversals can be composed one with the other with the result that the reversal of *"ip"* is *"pi,"* and if asked for the reversal of the reversal of *"ip"* produces *"ip"* again. Such games of course, can be expanded. We leave to our readers these interesting and important exercises.

Looking at two written syllables such as *ap* and *ip* it becomes possible to name the operation representing a passage from one to the other as *substitution.* If we substitute *i* for *a* or *a* for *i* we generate the other in the pair of syllables. Teachers can ask their students without giving anything away: "If you substitute in *ap* the blue for the beige, what will you get?" or "If you first form the pair brown/white, and substitute the red-rose for the white, what will you get?"

"Can anyone tap out *"ip"* on the Fidel (or on the chalkboard array)? Now reverse it. What sound will you make? Can you tap it out?"

Such exercises combine substitution and reversal and therefore represent intellectual games that may well challenge and excite young beginners.

Still with the brown one being the only consonant, another kind of blending offers itself.

Because their vowel is the same, *"pu"* and *"up"* can be blended by making students say faster and faster *"pu-up"* until there is only one merged utterance (we shall call it a *beat)* which is *"pup."*

Practicing on the other pairs — always uttering second the syllable beginning with the vowel — we get four more blendings yielding:

"pap" *"pip"* *"pep"* *"pop"*

If we return to the word *pup* we can cover one of the consonants and yield either *pu* or *up* as a result. Relating either to *pup* will allow us to introduce another intellectual operation we denote as *addition: pu* yields *pup* by addition, but also *up* yields *pup* by addition. At least we can use this language instead of saying, as many do, that we blend *p* (called *"pea"* or *"pə")* to *"up"* or *"pu."*

When these few words are written with colored chalks on the board we can open Book R_1 on page 28 and 29 and find there a number of the elements met in the previous lessons. The five vowels, the consonant *p;* the ten syllables above; the five words (this time because they are English we drop the quotation marks).

We also find a set of sequences which when sounded properly will evoke that we are concerned with English, *pop up* and *up up up* can well trigger the usual meaning at once.

What matters for us is that the purely functional exercises we engaged in, suddenly seem to go far beyond their scope. English makes its appearance unexpectedly.

From now on, this will be the case and only occasionally and for specific purposes shall we allow sequences of signs and of sounds without English meaning to be included in our presentations.

Another consonant *t* will be written on its own below the known vowels and given a treatment similar to that given to *p. t* is given the color magenta to signify its sound is different from that of *p.* In using the pointer to join *t* with the vowels, two of the syllables formed, *at* and *it,* are English words. We can then make the phrase *"at it."* Words can be formed such as *tat, tit, tut, tet, tot* which belong to the English language even if not all of them are familiar to beginners.

It is important to note that we are not yet leaving the technical aspects of reading to entertain ideas which are current in education courses and which concern content. We aim all the time at *mastery* in what we are doing, therefore we cannot allow ourselves to bring into the picture preconceived ideas, that may be appealing for one reason or another, but certainly will distract us from achieving the mastery which is possible with learners (already conversant with the notion of mastery). Beginning readers are people who have done a great deal on their own as proved by all the skills they acquired at that stage. They certainly know what it is to be intimately involved in meeting challenges and, so long as what they are doing makes sense to them, they will be mobilized by the prospect of mastery through exercises and through practice.

Hence, our austere but clear treatment of the subject, which leads to applying what has already been conquered in order to conquer further challenges.

Now we can bring together the five vowels and the two consonants studied and first give two shapes to both (*p* and *pp* for one and as *t* and *tt* for the other), so the array looks like this:

a u i e o
p t
pp tt

Then form as many combinations as possible that sound English through using the techniques used earlier. This will yield:

pat tap apt / pot top opt

pit tip / pet / putt / pitt

which, along with the few words already met, allow statements like:

- top it up - tip it up - tap it

We do not need to worry that little can be done with the same set of sounds and signs introduced this far. We shall soon experience an explosion and in fact, we have already achieved a great deal in terms of the manner in which we set about conquering English reading and writing. A beachhead is now available and that is what matters at this stage.

In the present study, called "R_1," we are concerned with the steps that will generate a strong awareness that we know what it is to read English. This is achieved through the intensive use of two instruments: Word Charts 1 and 2 and the Book R_1. To test the extent of the mastery, Worksheets #1 and #2 will be used.

The words on Charts 1 and 2 are found in Appendix A with those of all the other charts studied later.

The vowel sounds included in R_1 are the five of R_o plus two additional ones. The consonant sounds included are the two already discussed (*p* and *t*) plus five more.

The signs are introduced in two steps. Table 1 is obtained by adding two sounds of *s* to what has already been studied, and Table 2 follows

a	*u*	*i*	*e*	*o*	*a*	*I*
	o	*e*				
		y				

p	*t*	*s*	*s*	*m*	*n*	*y*
pp	*tt*		*ss*	*mm*	*nn*	
		ˊs	*ˊs*	*ˊm*		

Among the vowels are included more than one spelling for the sound at the beginning of *"up" (u* and *o)* and of *"it" (i, e,* and *y)* and two new vowel sounds:

> the indefinite article *a* (sounded as a "schwa" and colored yellow)
>
> the first person subject pronoun *I* (the only capital in the program) and given two colors to correspond to its two blended sounds.

In the consonant section are added five new sounds:

> for the last sound in —

"is" (*s and ´s*)

"us" (*s, ss, and ´s*)

"am" (*m, mm, and ´m*)

"in" (*n and nn*)

with a few of their forms and for the beginning sound in —

"yet" (y)

* * *

What we called an explosion takes place as soon as the third consonant *s* (the one in *is)* is introduced. For although only two English words *as* and *is* can be given here, we can now make a number of sentences that are complete — longer and more exciting than those we could produce so far — for example:

- is it as it is

- pat is as apt as pitt is

When the second sound of *s* (the one in *us)* is introduced (with a different color) a great deal more can be done.

- is it pat's pot

- it is

- set it up pat

- pat sets it up

- *pat upsets pop's pot*
- *pat upsets pop*
- *is pat as upset as pitt*
- *pass it pat*

Of course, when we are working in the way we suggested, a great deal more is given to the students to do and they seem to return the trust by becoming creative.

When Chart 1 is hung up on the wall and is used (as we shall explain below) it remains there for the students to look at and to be stimulated by. When Chart 2 joins it and is worked on in class (as we shall describe below) the opportunities to do more increase still and if students are given a chance they can make important discoveries.

Before we move any further, let us note that already in Chart 1 we have encountered the two ambiguities of written English, namely:

> two different sounds associated with the same shape

is and *us*

> more than one spelling (shape) for the same sound

us, pass, and *pat's*

Chart 1 is hung up on the wall.

The teacher who has so far only worked on the chalkboard and with the rectangle Fidel, touches with the pointer a certain sign (say *a* in *at)* and asks students to come up and point at other examples containing that sound. *pat, tap, sap, sat, as, apt, asset* are there to be touched.

Similar exercises with the other four vowels *i, e, u, o* will ensure:

1 that color is a guide,

2 that the representative of a sound is seen whether it is at the beginning, in the middle or at the end of a word, and

3 that the mind can stress what is asked for, and can ignore what is not required.

Once this recognition is accomplished, the words are looked at in a certain order to lead to a progressive mastery of the different items concerned.

If we begin with *it* and then relate *it* to *is* by substitution of the consonant *t* by the consonant *s* (we also call this "the curly purple" in contradistinction to "the curly green") we can form two sentences

- *it is* and *is it.*

as is obtained from *is* by a substitution of vowels. — *as is* is a phrase, — *as it is* a sentence, and — *is it as it is* another sentence.

All this is done by the teacher pointing silently. It is for the students to produce the sounds and if wanted, to write the statement down.

The "Game of Transformation" and the "Gap Game" can already appear at this level, if we want to use them.* The second is less dynamic and can be used as a starting point.

Writing on the chalkboard

p ___ *t*

the teacher asks students to find what may be put in the gap between *p* and *t*. Once a solution is given the student who suggested it may be asked to point to it on the word chart.

The next game, called the "Game of Location," goes hand in hand with *word reading* — that is the decoding of each of the 36 words on Chart 1. Teachers can introduce it by quickly covering any one of the words already decoded and asking "What did I cover?" If students give an answer or answers, these can be checked by uncovering the word just long enough for a quick look. If no one knows which word it is, students are given the same "quick look" in order to say what the word is.

We mentioned earlier how reversal, substitution, addition, have been used to generate new words. We must add *insertion* and

---

* cf. In Chapter 6, "Game of Transformation" pages 176-182 and "Gap Game" pages 175-176.

distinguish it from addition, in that the sound (or sign) is not placed at either end of the word, but in between two of its signs. For example *pat* becomes *past,* and *pet* becomes *pest.* Since these four operations link words in Chart 1 so that we can now ask students to go from one word to another — chosen because it requires only *one* change from the first — and ask them to name which one of the operations links the two words.

Then the longer game can be introduced. Two words on the chart can be chosen which are quite different from one another, and students can be asked to work out how they can go from the first to the second by going through other words on the chart, being careful each time to choose next a word that is made by *one* change from the preceding word (and also to one that is English should they construct one which is not there). For example:

1 to go from *as* to *pest* using these operations we propose one of the following routes:

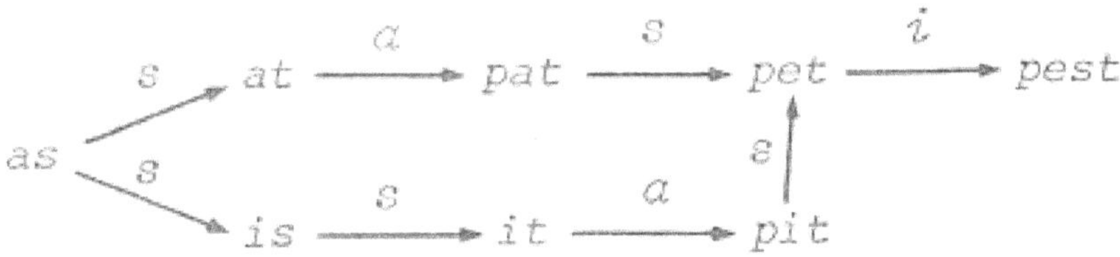

where $\xrightarrow{a}$ stands for *addition*

$\xrightarrow{s}$ for *substitution*

$\xrightarrow{i}$ for *insertion*

2 from *us* to *apt*

us $\xrightarrow{s}$ *as* $\xrightarrow{s}$ *at* $\xrightarrow{i}$ *apt*

Here we do not need to count the change of the second sound when we go from *us* to *as* be cause of an *equivalence* due to the fact that the shape *s* is the same even though it does not have the same sound in the two words;

3 from *as* to *steps*

as $\xrightarrow{s}$ *at* $\xrightarrow{a}$ *pat* $\xrightarrow{s}$ *pet* $\xrightarrow{a}$ *pets* $\xrightarrow{r}$ *step* $\xrightarrow{a}$ *steps*

where $\xrightarrow{r}$ stands for *reversal.*

In Worksheet #1 there are a few examples to be worked out of the Gap Game and of the Game of Transformations. We refer teachers to these if they wish to have some readymade examples to present to their students.

* * *

Now that the readers know how we constructed a word chart — using mainly algebraic operations — we can present more systematically what we do in our class lessons and how we use the Book R_1 to ensure mastery of the reading process as it may be encountered for the first time in English.

We already alluded to the visual dictation executed with the pointer on the rectangle Fidel. The same work can be done with the signs found on Tables 1 or 2 in the book, once the table is transferred to the chalkboard, or with a small pointer on the tables in the book. We use this method to generate words and we call it *Visual Dictation #1.*

But because sentences are made of words we can also point to a sequence of words on Charts 1 and 2 that form a sentence and ask students to utter them at the speed of speech, and with the phrasings and intonations required by some of the meanings.

In the classroom the signs on Tables 1 and 2 may be placed on the chalkboard using colored chalks. Moving with the pointer from one sign to another, we make words — at first slowly enough to ensure complete grasp by each of the students, then increasing the speed to generate words and sentences. When we shift to making sentences by *Visual Dictation #1,* again at first we go slowly and then speed up as the students show their capacity to move faster.

This of course will also be valid for *Visual Dictation #2* which is the name we give to moving the pointer from one word to another on the charts to give them an order that forms phrases or sentences.

Before we put the Book R_1 in the students' hands, we form sentences by *Visual Dictation #2* on Charts 1 and 2 — used separately or together. Many examples are given in R_1 and many many more can be formed.

One important game concerns the difference between the spoken and the written language. Intonation is in the voice and easily objectified by the energy available in the spoken language. In the written form it is not always possible to indicate it except by using additional words. For example *stop pat stop* can be sounded differently according to the following prefaces:

1 say it softly, or

2 say it being irritated, or

3 say it as a warning, or

4 say it as a caress, or

5 say it as a prayer, or

6 say it shouting to request stopping, or

7 say it jokingly, or

8 say it frightened, or

9 whisper it as when exhausted.

To convey such awarenesses does not require a vast written vocabulary. Young children living in an environment where all sorts of people express themselves have already acquired a certain amount of experience of what can be done with one's voice as an energy emitter and with intonation to convey some affective components that accompany verbalization. We do not have to wait long as they are becoming readers to bring to their notice examples of this kind already met within R_1.

Word Chart 2 joins Chart 1 on the wall. The teacher selects a word that can introduce *m*. Its sound is heard at the beginning of *mat* or at the end of *am*.

If *am* is chosen, its first sound is known from *at* and *as*. But the choice could be as easily: *sam* reached by substitution from *sat,* or *pam* and *mat* both reached from *pat,* or *met* from *set,* and so forth.

If *am* is the choice then *sam* and *pam* result. Either can be found by addition from *am* or from each other by substitution. A reversal makes *pam* into *map,* and a substitution leads into *mop* which with an addition becomes *mops. mop* by substitution becomes *mom* which by substitution yields *tom. tim* follows by substitution as does *tam,* which yields first *tamp* — and then *tamps* and next *stamps,* or then *stamp* and next *stamps.* If *met* is known, *mat* follows. But of course *met* yields easily *mess* and then *miss. pump* comes from *pup* by insertion; *mump* follows by substitution and *mumps* by addition.

us generates *must* that yields *mast* and *mist. I* is introduced separately and involved in sentences such as:

I sat up at pat's *I met tim at tom's* *I spot pat*

a (with the sound of schwa) is introduced in turn and involved in sentences such as:

it is a stop *is it a mess* *spot is a pup*

In a similar way we can introduce *n* as it sounds at the beginning of *not* and at the end of *in*. *pet* yields *net* which reversed yields *ten*. This opens two routes: *men* is reached by substitution and yields *man* by substitution, or *tent* is reached by addition and yields *sent* by substitution and then *spent* by insertion.

Of course, *in, an* or *on* could each serve as well to introduce *n*.

From *an* we would get *man* by addition and many others by substitution and so forth. Note then *sum* is derived from *sam* and *sun* from *sum* while *son* is a new spelling needed to be introduced separately.

The bottom line of Chart 2 cannot be derived as easily. So we show first *tem* by covering the *pt* at the end, and read that beat by going by substitution of *m* for *n* on the word *ten*. Then uncover the sound *p* to make *temp,* and quickly uncover the remainder to gain *tempt*. *attempt* follows easily but *assistant* needs to be treated as follows.

sit by insertion becomes *sist* and is quickly transformed into *assist*. *ant* becomes *ənt* when the yellow a replaces the beige one. Blending these two beats, we get this long word.

Each step in the learning of one or two words can be interleaved with sentences involving the new word or words.

sam sat on a pump	*it is not mumps*
I miss miss pam	*it is a must*

I am an assistant *tim tempts pat*

The sentences that are given in R_1 can be as extensive, in reference to life situations as can be associated with the vocabulary feasible with the signs/sounds on Table 2.

Some can be comic:

an ant in sam's pants

or

it is a pin in sam's pants

or

I'm not a nut, I'm a man

Some can be solemn:

ten stamps tempt pam

or

at ten, tim is not a man

Some can be factual:

tommy is tom's son

or

ten men sat on ten stumps in a tent

or

mom sent pants, pop stamps, tim pens, sam pens, pat nuts

or

I'm pat's assistant

Some can be moody:

sam is a pest, tom a nut

or

a yam is yummy

or

pam is in a mess

and so on, showing that it is possible to remain elementary with beginners yet neither shallow nor patronizing.

How complex and elaborate we shall be, will depend on the composition of our class and the stage of the work. Common sense advises us to aim all the time at a level of reading commensurate with the level of the spoken language. One way of achieving this is in what we have been suggesting here and demonstrated in the sentences in R_1.

Since we cannot all at once learn how to transcribe experience expressible in words in their written form, we must do the work progressively. But since a restricted vocabulary is not equivalent to poor language, we can offer our beginner students the keys to making as sophisticated sentences as they can think of or imagine, with the 80 or so words on Charts 1 and 2.

A good exercise for teachers is to list as many sentences as come to their own mind with the words on the two charts and all those that can be generated with the signs and sounds referred to in Table 2.

Our collection in R_1 can serve as an example, but there are many, many more.

* * *

There are subtle but elementary observations about the English language that can be started within "R_1." On Word Chart #1, we give two s signs for the plural and two ´s signs for the possessive. By listening carefully to what they themselves say, or what others say, students can notice that words ending in *p* or *t* require the green *s* while those ending in *m* or *n* require the purple one.

Thus *step* makes *steps* and *pant, pants* with the green *s* while *mom* makes *mom's* and *sun* makes *suns* with the purple one. Students' pointing at the proper signs on the charts will tell whether that awareness has been reached.

We shall have to wait till we reach Chart #4 to make the plurals of *pass, miss* and *mess.*

* * *

To sum up the work of "R_1" we can say that the most important step has been the generation of the certainty that the activities of "R_0," when applied to the combination of some vowels and some syllables, generate the written English language — a non-negligible amount of which can be met with as small a vocabulary as is contained in Word Charts 1 and 2.

In our earlier writings we spoke of the *first certificate of reading* when students knew how to read what could be done through Visual Dictation #1 on the signs of Table 1 and through Visual Dictation #2 on what is today Word Chart #1. In our revised edition of the materials of *Words in Color* we have extended the beginners' grasp to cover what can be done with Visual Dictation #1 on Table 2 and with Visual Dictation #2 on Charts 1 and 2. *Still we consider the work done on "R_1" the cornerstone of all the future work* which can be looked at as expansions of what is covered under R_1.

However essential such expansions are for the ultimate goal of reading everything in the English language, the foundations of the ability to become a fluent and competent reader are in R_1 and these need all our attention.

As presented, the foundations go beyond the assimilation of the conventions handled thoroughly in R_0. They involve the introduction of the syllables and of the two ambiguities of English. At the same time as they show clearly that it is possible to establish a two-way traffic between the spoken language —

already highly developed in young students — and the written one we are trying to give them. We are consciously leading our beginners to the awareness that they can own two almost isomorphic systems of code meanings: the spoken code already second nature in them, and the written code. The latter makes only a few additional demands on students until they reach the point much later of realizing that they can use the written word to expand their experience.

In terms of awareness, "R_1" is so important that we give it the same extension as we do to "R_2" or "R_3." "R_2" is concerned with all the sounds of English, while "R_3" focuses on all the forms (or spellings) of all the English sounds. In fact no real mastery of "R_2" and "R_3" is possible without that assumed in "R_1." What we want students to master in "R_1" is mainly qualitative — that is, concerned with deeper awareness. We state that this depth is not beyond beginners of ages 4—6 and that it is a requirement of a common sense approach to give children of that age as much exposure of this universe (of "R_1") as can be conceived possible without our having any fear of confusing them.

The instruments described in this chapter tell clearly what we know to be possible.

5 Reading and Writing What we Can Say, New Awarenesses

In Chapter 7 we shall consider various purposes of reading. For example, the use of textbooks to acquire knowledge. In this chapter we give ourselves a more limited but a definite task. We consider the needs of people who speak a language and who want —

1 to put on paper what they know they can say, and

2 to extract from a text as much meaning as they would from a set of statements spoken in a conversation with them.

To make this still more definite, it seems reasonable to us to work specifically on two cardinal awarenesses — needed by students in order to be free to forge ahead in their studies of and through their mother tongue.

- The *first awareness* is that all the sounds they can produce have been given a written form and that

English isolates 59 such sounds and gives them at least one sign each.

- The *second awareness* is that in order to write down all the words of English, over 400 forms for the 59 sounds have been used, and that these forms (or signs) in various combinations and permutations form the written English language.*

By now our readers must be clear that in this book we are writing of "programs" only to make our exposition simpler. Our first concern at all times is with awareness and the subordination of teaching to learning in the fields of reading and writing, rather than with our own ideas and how teachers have to implement them. The content of this Chapter does indeed refer to an unfolding of a way of working connected with primer books, classroom materials, and student worksheets but, we insist, this is done solely because we have created a technology that makes possible the all important subordination of teaching to learning in these fields.

In the previous chapter, we already introduced under "R_1," the techniques and types of materials which are part of that technology. "R_2" and "R_3" both use similar materials and expand by stages what "R_0" and "R_1" have given our students. "R_2" and "R_3" can therefore be a natural sequel to what we did earlier and integrate the ways of working met thus far so that students will not experience shock when the set of charts is added to, or a new

---

* In fact when computing the number of signs, we have excluded several which are needed for geographical places or people's names.
(Editor's Note: 1977 edition charts have 58 sounds. The 59th sound, *z* as in *schizo* and *zz* as in *pizza*, was added in 2010.)

book is handed out. A quick look at the two books R_2 and R_3, will show that the format of R_1 is preserved*: new signs for both new and old sounds appear at the top of the even numbered pages, and under them sample words are given which include these signs (using the sounds being introduced) but without any indication of their meaning. These words are collected here for a number of purposes. One of these is to stimulate students to find more words using these signs, and another is to provide words from which sentences can be formed of the type found on the odd numbered pages through which a meaning is attached to the words.

Both books contain Tables of signs from the larger sound/sign Fidel which serve as a summary of each stage in the more gradual introduction of new sets of signs. In R_2 Tables 3, 4, and 5 focus on new sounds in a certain number of the forms given them in English. In R_3, Tables 6 and 7 complete the unfolding of the total set of signs needed to write all English words. Table 7 is the complete Fidel given in black and white.**

Both books contain short passages for continuous reading. While the odd numbered pages show sentences for practice of reading and writing, these sentences are deliberately unconnected. The paragraphs of the stories show how sentences brought together produce some effect characteristic of stones. In stories, sentences sustain each other and add something needed to create a climate, to convey more information, or to permit the writer to make a point.

---

* Editor's Note: New editions of the Reading Primers may not follow the described format.

** In the previous editions of *Words in Color* a special booklet no longer obtainable — the *Word Building Book* — contained 16 Tables instead of 7.

These two books use a different size type to convey to the students that they have graduated when they passed from "R_2" to "R_3." Now they can read smaller type; that is cope with more information per page. The end of R_3 includes some pages which are given either

1 to a summing up of what has been achieved through the work covered by R_o to R_3 and the techniques used in the classroom lessons, or

2 to what is considered common sense at that moment;

that is, the introduction of elements belonging to the culture rather than to the language such as capitals, all the signs of punctuation, and the names of the letters or the alphabet. For instance, it is common sense not to introduce capitals during R_o to R_3 so as not to burden newcomers to learning reading and writing with what may confuse or distract them. This is particularly so because the capitals can be learned far more quickly and easily at the end of the course — and be learned without any need to ever go over them again.

In the body of R_2 and R_3, we continue to use the sans serif cursive type which corresponds most closely to the typeface adopted on the charts. In the last stories of the *Book of Stories* we meet for the first time the Roman type found in most texts, newspapers and magazines.

In Chapter 4 we spoke of Visual Dictation #1 which produces out of the colored signs of the chalkboard array (or the larger sound/sign Fidel) the words of English we need to form sentences. Some of these words are gathered on the word charts, and the making of sentences with the pointer from these words we called Visual Dictation #2. When we point out sentences one after the other to form stories, we speak of Visual Dictation #3, even if this happens infrequently in the textbooks in contrast to the other two Visual Dictations.

These dictations are an essential technique. They are done silently by the teachers who can continuously test that their students are doing the work of reading properly. This means that not only do they say what each word tells them to say but also they run the words together in the proper phrasings required, they put the stresses and intonations required and produce a good melody of English.

Through silent teaching and the sounding by the students, we aim at giving teachers and students their respective responsibilities. We are not concerned yet with silent reading or speed reading. Before anything else, we must secure that the students know what they are doing and do it as well as they can. In the temporal hierarchy of learning, the encounter of each of the sounds and of some of their written forms must be done systematically without lumping them together, but also without any waste of time. The format of two pages in the book described above: — words on the left and sentences on the right — tells us also how to proceed in the classroom lessons. At a certain moment in a lesson we add one new chart to those already on the wall and put it next to the last in the order of numeration (printed in red on the bottom white border). For "R_2" the set will go from Charts 3 to 10. For "R_3" the set extends from Charts 11 to 20.

"R_2"

Chart 3 introduces in lavender *f* (of *fun)* and *ff* (of *puff),* in olive the *f* (of *of),* in green *d* (of *dad),* in pink *y* (of *yes*), in light purple the *th* (of *the),* and in a pale green *th* (of *path*). The red-rose *y* is not new but is available now on the charts for adding to the end of many words. It was met for the first time in R_1 (and Table 2) in words like *puppy,* and occurs on this chart also in *fifty*. All of the words on the chart that contain the new sounds (colors) can be decoded by the students so long as *one* word containing the new sound is given by the teacher (or by some student who happens to know it) as was done in Chapter 4. In the case of the *f* (of *of),* this word is the only example on the chart, and therefore it must be given.

There are more words containing these sounds and signs on pages 2—12 of R_2 and of course a number of sentences that can also serve to show teachers what they can do with these words. Naturally, if some of these sentences are "borrowed" by the teacher as examples for Visual Dictation #2 during the lessons, the students will meet them later in the book among many others that are possible with the vocabulary of the first 3 charts.

The ease with which so many more sentences can be made will become apparent as soon as teachers ask their students to use Visual Dictation #2 themselves

1 to produce their own sentences, and

2 to point out one or more of these sentences to be judged by their peers.

The most exciting sentences can be written, read, and kept carefully on the chalkboard before the pages of R_2 are looked at. The flow of words corresponding to these sentences must be the one that corresponds to spoken speech. This will help to convey meaning. There are opportunities offered teachers by the mere fact that these words and no others were selected for Chart #3. The choice has been influenced by the concept of *transformation* which generates new words

1 from words on previous charts, or

2 from words on the new chart.

For example, *it* gives *fit* and *at, fat.* One of them can serve as the first word to introduce *f.* From one or the other, the few words in lavender can be deduced. But *an* can serve as well by letting us begin with *fan* from which we can obtain both *fat* and *fun* by substitution. From *fat, fit* can be obtained by substitution and then *fist* by insertion; and *fast* can be added by substitution. Returning to *it* we get *if* by substitution. From *pup* we pass to *puff* and from these to *stuff* which can be decoded by covering the first sign to get *tuff* (which one day will be written *tough)* and uncovering it to find *stuff.* From *stuff* and *if* we can form *stiff* and change it into *sniff* by substitution. *fifty* can also be found through knowing *if*, which enables us to see both "fif" or "ift" by addition and merge them into *fift,* and add the red-rose *y* for the final beat. *fifth* easily follows from "fif."

The sound of *th* found in *fifth* is also given in *path, math* and *thin* and can be introduced from *pass* by putting the tongue between the teeth while uttering the final sound.

It is obvious that there is no reason for not introducing any number of sentences alternating with these decoding exercises by using words from Charts 1 and 2 along with those already decoded on Chart 3.

> pat is fun, tom is fit, it is a fist, mom is fast, sniff it sam, a fan is a pump, tom puffs and sniffs, pam stuffs sam's pants.

of needs a special handling since it is the only word with that consonant. The vowel has the sound value represented by the deep yellow color in Chart 2 in a and in "assistant" and "attempt" and on Chart 3 in *e* that is part of the word *the.*

As soon as *of* is introduced by the teacher, it is possible to make sentences and phrases like *of mom's, of men not of pumps, son of man, a tent of net stuff,* etc. The word *tennis* has the first *nn* on the charts (though it was presented in Table 2). From it *funny* can be formed with *fun* and the ending *-y* found on this chart, and lead to *tennis pants, men of tennis, tennis map. messy* can be formed from *mess* and lead to *a messy tent, messy* *pam, a messy mess. sunny* can be derived and used in phrases such as, *a sunny spot.* But more urgently, the introduction of the words with *d* such as *and, dad,* and *did* are anticipated to generate interesting developments. Assuming that *and* is derived from *an, end* follows and then *sand* and *send, stand* and *mend* are easily derived. *ad* and *add* can follow, with *sad, mad* and *dad* coming soon after. *did* and *dud,* as well as *mud* and *dust* (this from *must*) follow easily and lead to a greater variety to sentences such as:

> dad stands on a pump, stand up tom, tom stands up, is dad sad, did sam stamp it, tom did turn it in, it is sad if tom is mad, pam stands up in mud, did dad send pam in

From *tess* we get *ted* and from it *fed.* Hence *mom is fed up as sam puffs and puffs.*

The introduction of the second *th* brings *the, this* and *that* again opening up new possibilities:

> the ten men sat in the tent as tess and pat sent sam in, this must stand up, and that's that.

On Chart 3, the three different soundings (colorings) of the ending *ed* for the past tense are brought in early since they too will make life more interesting because of the variety of thoughts they permit.

sum and *thin*   require the first *ed*

(along with the doubling of the consonant) to make *summed* and *thinned*

sniff and *pump* require the second *ed*

to make *sniffed* and *messed, stop* and *mop* do also (along with the doubling of the consonant) to make *stopped* and *mopped*

mend and *dust* both require the third

ed to make *mended* and *dusted.*

By covering the *e* of the first *ed* we make available the required *d* needed later for *love* to become *loved.* By covering the *e* on the second *ed* we have the *d* needed later for *like* to become *liked.*

How long it takes to go through all this work is a function of the situation in the classroom. It may be done in one or two lessons with groups of students who love their work and show themselves to be swift learners. It may take five lessons if the teacher wishes to be thorough and do many, many exercises to be sure that everybody gets everything. It may take weeks if the work is done at a slow pace and a wide variety of exercises, such as those indicated in the worksheets, are stretched over the lessons.

Whatever the duration of the lessons for the integration of the material on Charts 1, 2, 3, the gains resulting from working on them will be felt in what comes after. It will be felt first, because the students can appreciate the variety of the work; second, because so much of the work can be creative and on an individual basis; and third, because the restrictions imposed by the choices of sounds so far — none of which are felt as imposed from the outside — create affinities between the words that produce a flow of sentences felt as a true current.

The classroom work will include what we have described above:

1 generation of many words on the chart through transformation from any *one* which the teacher uttered to introduce a new sound;

2 the forming of other words that could be made by transformation but are not given on the chart;

3 looking at the words on the even numbered pages of *R2*;

4 constructing sentences by Visual Dictation #2;

5 looking at the sentences on the odd numbered pages of *R2*;

6 letting students make their own sentences out of the words on the charts;

7 adding to these, words found in #2 above;

8 reading aloud of the "best" sentences;

9 gathering these sentences;

10 oral dictation of some sentences;

11 examining by the students of their production, comparing it to what can be shown by pointing at words on the charts or by Visual Dictation #1 on the Fidel, that would serve as means of correction when needed;

12 working on the various sections of the worksheets corresponding to these three charts;

13 collective examination of individual work.

With this kind of dynamics available in the classroom many of the discipline problems met in schools will vanish and be replaced by excitement, interest and progress on all the fronts involved. In particular, fast learners do as much as they wish; slow learners can take their time and while doing very well on what they work on, they increase their own speed of learning because they now have criteria, know exactly what is asked of them and not bound by a performance beyond their capabilities.

As we shall have occasion to stress in various parts of this text, the game-like activities suggested — which are self-motivating, varied, and growing in complexity — do give students constant opportunities to work cooperatively with their peers. A grateful teacher receives their gifts as tokens of where they are and what they are doing with themselves. Continuous feedback is now possible and teacher and student affect each other for the benefit of all. Learning becomes what matters to the teacher and is experienced by the students as expansion of their mental powers. The lessons are empirical sessions in which no one tries to please others and instead enjoys being stretched beyond what the earlier challenges made possible.

In fact, more and more can be done as new charts are introduced and integrated with the previous ones. What actually happens is that the presence of new sounds and new signs, which are part of the expanded set now contemplated, operate at a higher level of integration subordinating what was there in order to do much more than was possible earlier. The lessons are demonstrations that growth is taking place, that the conquests continue and will gradually involve all this is needed to be on top of written English and its demands. Confidence results from proof of one's increased competence, and not from the teacher's appreciation of one's success.

For example, when Chart 4 is added to the first three a new explosion is experienced. Now again a great deal more can be done that one wished one could do. This new opening is experienced as another breakthrough which will let much more of the written language appear.

Essentially there are only two new sounds on it: one carried by the royal blue *l* (or *ll)* and one by the aqua *w,* both heard as part of a syllable in which they appear. A double colored sign *ll* (yellow/blue) appears which contain a vowel and is therefore a syllable, and makes possible the utterance of the contraction *I'll* which brings colloquial speech into one's writing.

We met *tt* and *ss* on Chart 1 (and 2), *ff* on Chart 3. Now on Chart 4 we meet *ll.* These are spellings occurring at the end of English words. There will one day be words ending in *rr* and some perhaps in *bb.* We introduce these endings here because of their frequency. Pairs of words like *tell* and *let* — each reverse the sound sequence of the other — and yet only one has a double ending; while *less* is the reverse of *sell,* and both have a double ending. One can note that *till* and *until* have contrasting spellings at the end, while *less* and *unless* do not. All of this will tell that we can offer the complexity of English for our students' scrutiny this early. Exercises can be given during classroom lessons to draw attention to these items of written English which later will be reviewed in the spelling lessons. Since they appear at the beginning of R_2 they convey our conviction that they are for beginners and indeed are better presented early and with their complexity rather than postponed — particularly when done in a natural manner through the word charts.

On pages 14-16 of R_2, we can find sufficient work for two or more lessons, giving enough practice with these two sounds. When the contents of the corresponding worksheets are added this will offer teachers material for another two or more hours of work.

For the first time on the last line of this chart (4) we see two words that have the same form when appearing without color, but whose difference in coloring indicates that they sound differently, and in this case have very different meanings: *wind* as a noun, and *wind* as a verb.

It is also the first time we find the sound that goes with the first person pronoun *I* as part of a word. Until now, in the first four charts (1-4) only the five vowels met in R_o have been used to introduce the consonants *p, t, s, m, n, f, d, th, th, y, l* and *w* along with the "schwa" a needed to convey unstressed vowels in English words and the *I* needed to make personal statements.

The latter is a useful device when language is seen as the means of expression.

Of course, the small number of sentences found in R_2 will be more and more only a token of what is possible with the increasing vocabulary found on the charts and on the even numbered pages of R_2. Hence, school work and homework will rely more and more on what the students find they can do with what has been revealed to them.

This is to be considered as one of the bonuses resulting from the way of working we call common sense. It will lead students towards greater independence from others, greater autonomy shown by increased initiative displayed in their work, and heightened sense of responsibility.

These three components of independence, autonomy and responsibility, together represent the freedom-to-work that teachers everywhere dream of giving their students. Through the techniques and materials of the subordination of teaching to learning, it is now achievable in the field of reading. It can already be felt at this early stage in the process of mastery.

In fact, it is obvious that if we aim at *mastery at every moment* in the acquisition of the hierarchy of skills needed to form a major skill such as reading or writing, we shall obtain mastery of the whole through the process of integration and subordination mentioned above. All we need to do is to be alerted to the existence of this way of working and to be sure of practicing it continuously.

In demanding that our students be able to do as much as possible with what we offered them under "R_0" and "R_1" we did give them their freedom from guessing at words and their own sense of responsibility with respect to

1 letting each word tell them what to say, and

2 letting their spoken language contribute stresses, phrasing, intonation and melody.

This is integrated in the way they utter a flow of words suggested by the scanning of each written sentence. From the correct performance of these disciplines, the comprehension made possible by their intelligence, their imagination, and their practice of their spoken language yields what is also called *comprehension through reading*. What we have done with Charts 3 and 4 and the first sixteen pages of R_2, supported by work in the classroom and through the worksheets, will extend these same attitudes as they meet the challenge of mastering the whole field "R_2." Hence, when we move on through Charts 5-10 we know that we are integrating material that aims at greater freedom and greater responsibility, and we insist upon feeling that we can do even more as we forge ahead. This more is not only quantitative — that is, concerned with a larger written vocabulary and a larger crop of sentences and stories — it is also qualitative by being more far-reaching, more shaded, and more subtle. Indeed, we have more opportunities all the time to be challenged by components of the language not being considered per se simply because we are giving our time to other aspects.

For instance, the appearance of the suffixes *-ly* on Chart 5 and *-ing* on Chart 6 give us the means of becoming aware *and* of practicing a large number of adverbs and adjectives and of verb forms we did not have the components to form before that. Teachers who have noticed that by simply hanging up one new chart after the other that an increased number of sounds can be obtained by using the means developed thus far, will sense that the two suffixes *-ly* and *-ing* are creators of a new kind of expansion in the use of the language and will seize the new opportunity. They may not find more than one or two examples in R_2, but they cannot escape seeing the presence of these endings on the charts and feel drawn to using them.

On page 19 of R_2 (related to Chart 5) we see the word *lovely*. This word is used in only one sentence on page 20. Looking at the five charts side by side with our mind taken by the opportunity of using *-ly* we may want our students to recognize, in their sensitivity, that only adjectives (or qualifiers; providers of properties) can stand being coupled with *-ly*. We can then make it a point in our lessons to find out whether that suffix can be placed at the end of words already familiar and on the Charts 1-5. Students being natives who have some experience of English, will soon reject "stoply" but accept "sadly," or "lively" and hesitate about "spotly." By participating as a class in a hunt for words formed in this way which can be accepted or rejected — or be considered doubtful — the students will clearly have the valuable experience of how some words *generate a feel* that they refer to attributes and qualities, while others do not. Revealing to students that they have the criteria in their sensitivity to the spoken language will relieve them of storing these in their memory. This will make a world of difference in their proper equipment as students of English. It can become second nature rather than being remembered or forgotten. When the words "adjective" or "adverb" are mentioned, one day they will serve to label real experiences rather than words retained through definition.

Similarly, when *-ing* is met on Chart 6. In English, verbs are among the most important words because they translate the active mode of thought of the culture and are used in preference to nouns, while say, in French, it is the opposite. This will be found at once because *fathering* and *mothering* will be recognized as English words and easily formed by words on the same line as *-ing* on Chart 6. But of course going back to Charts 1-5 will suggest an enormous crop. So many English words can be used when they may be thought of first as displaying another function, like *pat* as a name and *top* as a noun which can also be used as verbs. The study of the effect of *-ing* at the end of words will at once

1 make so many more words available — almost doubling the vocabulary on the charts,

2 suggest the need for doubling of some consonants in words before *-ing* is added on,

3 give opportunity to use the continuous present in the formation of sentences,

4 reveal that one form of the verb accepts *-ing* while others do not — thus bringing awareness of the link between the stem of a verb, the imperative form, and the present indicative form, while

separating them from the forms used to express the past,

5 contrast what happens in spelling with verbs ending in *e* when for the past tense *d* alone is added to make the needed *ed* ending *(love* becomes *loved)* while when *-ing* is added the *e* must be dropped (*love* becomes *loving*).

Since *is* has been used from Chart 1, *am* from Chart 2, *was* from Chart 4, and *were* from Chart 5, the availability of the suffix *-ing* can allow the formation of statements that express shades of meaning about the present and the past. *do* appearing on Chart 6, while *did* was on Chart 3, *doing* will be available from now on for many sentences.

In addition to the suffixes just discussed, Chart 5 is obviously used to familiarize students with the sounds associated with *r* and *k* as consonants, and with the new vowel sound found in the word *fur*. The spellings met are *re, ck, ke, ne, me, le, y, a, o, e,* colored to refer to new sounds or those introduced previously. Words like *my, any,* can be easily decoded because of color and add further articulation in the composition of sentences. Words like, *time, like, love, ask, word, find* are welcome since they open new worlds for expression.

Chart 6, besides introducing the sounds represented by *h* in *has* as well as the *o* of *do* and the *u* of *put,* also gives the contractions *don't, won't, -'ve,* and *-n't* which make it possible to transcribe colloquial language. The first example of *g* as sounded in *give* appears.

Out of these two charts we can offer expansions that everyone will welcome. As soon as *r* is introduced we notice that this sound in English has three values according to whether it begins a word, ends it, or is somewhere in the middle. *r* when blended with a vowel distorts it. We could have given *r* three shades of color but it seemed more in keeping with the phonetic tradition found in dictionaries to add four vowels and give each of them one of four colors that distinguish them from the other ones. On Chart 6, we meet one of them in the words *fur, were, word,* and *world.* On the same Chart 6 we meet another one in the word: *there.* But we have to wait for Chart 7 to see a third one in the words: *or, for, nor,* etc. and for Chart 9 to meet the one in the words: *are, car, far,* etc.

The colors chosen for these vowels will ensure

1 that the schwa followed by *r* (we have given the schwa a deep yellow color) — as in *mother* — is not to be confused with the sound of *e* in *her,*

2 that the *o* in *for* is pronounced differently from the *o* in *off* (Chart 8),

3 that the sound for *e* in *there* is differently pronounced from that of *e* in *set,*

4 that the sound of *a* in *car* or *father* is very differently pronounced from that of *a* in *cab.*

On the last line of Chart 6, in the words *don't* and *won't,* the so-called "long" *o* appears for the first time.* The useful words, *from, little, but, by* and *been* are also introduced on Chart 6. Thanks to them many sentences can be added to the numerous ones already possible.

The three forms *to, too* and *two* are also found on Chart 6. Sentences like *give two to him too* are now possible and will serve to distinguish them. One exercise of significance can be started with Charts 5 and 6 and used after that when returning to the earlier charts or moving to the following ones. For example the word *mind* on Chart 5 can be seen as related to *find* (on the same chart) and to *wind* (in the previous one) by substitution. The words *kind, rind, hind, bind,* can be formed as easily and considered known from now on. From *food* (on Chart 6) we can form *mood* or *fool.* Students could be able to work out similar exercises on other selected words.

On page 30 of R_2 we find the first two short stories. The first has seventy-four words and the second, sixty-four. They can only appear at this point because of the choice made on Charts 1-5 of not using the so-called "long" vowels — except for the word "I." Since the words in these two stories are mainly monosyllabic, they do not offer any obstacle to our request for continuous reading at the speed of speech. It may be advisable to work on a few words separately and before looking at the stories: *myself, tiger, prefer, planning* in the first story and on *sometimes* and *parents* found in the second story. A good way of assisting

---

* In fact, it has been given two colors and is a diphthong.

students in giving the stories the phrasing of speech is to place a light pencil mark to indicate those pauses *not* represented by punctuation.

Such markings could be considered a technique of this course which definitely helps students become aware of the importance of phrasing and intonation in reading — and results in considerable consequence for comprehension.

Let us note in passing that the two stories on page 30 are preceded for the first time by *two* pages of sentences using words similar to those on Charts 5 and 6. On page 27 examples of words containing *o* as in *go* and *no* are given and used in the subsequent sentences. Most of the so-called "long" vowels are studied on Chart 7 and on page 36 and those following in R_2.

The first line of Chart 6 ends with *hat,* that of Chart 7 starts with *hate.* When the charts are hung up near each other the contact of these two words and their contrast may serve to help students remember that "generally" the presence of a *mute e* at the end of a word alters the value of the preceding vowel.

Chart 7 is the one on which we chose to introduce the rest of so-called "long" vowels which are in reality two sounds blended into a diphthong (except *e* as in *be).* We have met the two-colored *I* and its two other forms *i* and *y* and the two-colored *o* (and the genuine long sound of *o* in *do).* Now we meet the two-colored *a*; the two-colored *u*, and the only real long vowel among them: *e.*

When reading Chart 7, we can consider it our opportunity to make our students acquainted with the fact that English has a larger number of vowels than the five of the alphabet. We met at first five (on Chart 1), then the schwa *ə* and *I*, then vowels affected by *r* and the two *oo*'s and now the remainder with two sounds each and *e* of *be*. Making a table would have been useful if we did not have the Fidel. So we can now find room on the walls of the classroom to hang the top Fidel Charts of vowels in the order of the numerals printed on their borders (1, 2, 3, 4).* The first chart shows only the sounds of vowels met on Chart 1. The second chart shows first in two columns the schwa. On that occasion we can say in passing, "There are this many forms in bright yellow because this sound is used a great deal in English — mainly when vowels are not stressed." Next to the schwa, we placed the vowel associated with a sound close to the schwa but much stronger. It is the one met in the word *word* and we gave it a salmon tint. Next to it comes the column for the sound of *a* in *all* (a brown shade), and the column for the sound of *a* in *father* (a purple shade). The next Fidel vowel chart refers to the *o* in *to* or *do* (in a deep green) in one column, and *e* (of *he)* in the second column (in vermillion). Then comes the sound for *ai* as in *fair* (in turquoise), the short sound of *oo* as in *look* (in grey brown), and the sound of *o* as in *for* (in dark brown).

The last vowel chart of the Fidel is made only of two-colored groups:

I (white over pink)

---

* It is best to choose a space tall enough so that the four consonant Fidel Charts can later be hung under the vowel charts to make Visual Dictation #1 possible on the Fidel.

a (sounded like the name of the letter; blue over pink)

o (sounded like the name of the letter; light brown over aqua)

u (sounded like the name of the letter, pink over dark green)

and in the last column:

ou of *out*	(purple over aqua) Word Chart 12 (page 64 of R_2)
oi of *oil*	(light brown over pink) Word Chart 17 (page 8 of R_3)
oi of *au revoir*	(aqua over purple) other examples such as: *memoirs, repertoire,* (page 58 of R_3)
o of *one*	(aqua over pale yellow)

The third vowel chart shows one two-colored group (pink over grey brown) for *you** in *your* which is shorter than the word *you.*

---

* Editor's Note: New editions of the Word Charts have separated the *y* from *ou* in *your*, eliminating two-colored signs in this word.

It is found also as *u* in *cure* and *curious* as well as *fury* and *furious* (page 36 of R_3).

Twenty-three columns for twenty-three vowels recognizable in English are shown on the Fidel, and are all, except the five less common two-colored groups, introduced by the end of Word Chart 7.

Pages 32 to 34 of R_2 serve in the study of the sounds on Chart 7. From then on we shall have at our disposal almost all the vowels and feel no restriction in this respect while introducing the last of the consonant sounds.

Let us note the two-color *r* of *iron* on Chart 7, and the strange form for the lilac *on* in the same word — strange because the *o is mute*. Mute letters are many in English. In fact, every letter of the alphabet can be mute in one or more words in English. The study of the truth of this statement can be the object of a lesson or so sometime during a school year. The significance of this study is experienced best when entering deliberately in the consideration of spelling as presented in R_3 (see also next chapter in this book).

On Chart 7 we meet some words whose aim is to answer questions that some teachers of reading have. For instance, in the word *bursts* there are four consonants one after the other, and this word is on the same line as *girl* and *hurt* that have only two together while *first* has three. Will students show that these words are equally easy to read because of the discipline of reading they acquired in R_o or will they show that when consonants replace vowels words are more difficult to decode.

The last line on that same chart proposes pinpointed challenges teachers may wish to settle early and quickly. Having met *give* and *go* will students read as easily *leg* and *egg* with this consonant at the end? Will they show that to put at the beginning of very similar words (such as *get* and *got*) or of a larger one — *globe* — may be sufficient to give the required experience with that consonant? If this is the case, we have learned something of significance in teaching reading. By placing *use* and *refuse* next to each other but with two different colors for *se,* we offer the opportunity to teachers of giving exercises from which students will infer whether these two words represent nouns or verbs. Others are given on page 38 of R_2. Note that words like "exercise" and "practice" do *not* require a change in sound (nor the spelling for the second, at least in American English) when evoking a verb or a noun. When integrating the words on Chart 7 with all the previous ones already met, we open to the students a further field for exploring some aspects of English while changing sentence-making into a broader skill.

The *e* (in red rose) which appears on that chart can serve to show how the mute *e* after a consonant of which there are so many examples on this chart must take on sound in order to produce new words such as the superlatives of adjectives *(cute* becomes *cutest),* such as certain plurals (*horse* becomes *horses*), and such as certain past tenses (*date* becomes *dated*) are introduced explicitly. Since this is not done in R_2 it must be taken up in lessons in the classroom. On page 40 of R_2 we find the third passage for continuous reading. The two signs of punctuation met earlier (the comma and the period) are the only ones still used, while on the stories of page 53, question marks and quotation marks made their appearance and on page 54, the exclamation mark.

Chart 8 proposes only one new sound, the nasal *n* since the *o* in *off, dog* and *gone* (vowel column 8 on the Fidel) was considered when the different sound of *o* in *for* appeared on Chart 7. This sound of *n* shows its contrast with its more usual sound in pairs of words like *hungry* and *hundred,* or *think* and *thin* (Chart 3).

On this same chart there are several new but common spellings for sounds already met which provide some unexpected contrasts in soundings: *does* contrasts with *goes; lost* with *most; done* and *gone* contrast with each other and both with *bone* (Chart 7); and *some* and *come* both contrast with *home* (Chart 7).

Words close in sound such as *dirty* and *thirty,* and also close in appearance such as *thirty* and *thirsty,* are also displayed on this chart. All in all the words on this chart encourage students to be more adventurous in the production of sentences, examples of which are found on pages 38, 39, and 44 of R_2.

On Charts 9 and 10 there are many more examples given of vowel columns 9 (as in *are)* and 12 (as in *air)* of the Fidel.

The consonant sounds* generally associated with *sh* and *ch* appear on Chart 9. Those with *j* in Chart 10. It is possible to do a very thorough study of these consonants at this level. The sign *sh* always refers to the same sound while *ch* appears in three colors to represent respectively the three sounds it has in *chin, michigan* (or *machine,* Chart 19) and *chorus.* The two most frequent spellings of the sound at the beginning of *chill* are *ch* and *tch* found on Chart 9, leaving for Chart 11 its spelling *t* as in *question.* The sound of *j* in *jack* is met with five of its eight spellings in *job, gym, soldier, judge* and *adjective,* — two more spellings (*ge* as in *age,* and *dg* as in *judgment)* appear on page 56 of R_2. The first word is found on Chart 12 while the second can easily be formed in class by starting with *judge* (Chart 10). The eighth spelling of *gg* (which appears on the Fidel) can be found later in *exaggerate* (Chart 15).

On Chart 10 the sound for *t* in *education* and *generation* appears and is given also on page 56 of R_2. This chart also contains the common word *all* (that is part of so many words *tall, fall, mall, hall, ball, call, small,* etc.) and introduces the first *x* as in *next* in two colors (gold over green). To this form *x,* English has associated four more sounds which we distinguish by color: *x* as in *xylophone* in one color (purple — same color as for *s* in *is);* *x* as in *exam* in two colors (grey over purple); *x* as in *anxious* in two colors (gold over blue); *x* as in *luxurious* in two colors (gold over indigo).

---

* Teachers may wish at this point to hang under the four Fidel Charts of vowels the four charts of consonants (in the order of the numerals printed on their border — 5, 6, 7, 8). Then it will be easy to locate on the Fidel the consonant sounds which we are proposing be introduced next on Word Charts 9, 10 and 11 as part of "R_2."

Although R_2 is dedicated to the collection of the sounds of English it has been useful to put in it items found in some of the charts that are beyond Chart 10. Thus on page 60 we find the double sound (gold over aqua, found on chart 11) associated with the two letters *qu* which are found together in so many words that *q* is never considered per se in English words. On page 64, the two different sounds associated with the same spelling *wh* as in *who* and in *why,* are introduced because of their frequent usage although they also only appear for the first time on Word Chart 11.

The vowel sound that appears for the first time in *mouth* (purple over aqua) on Chart 11, and in profusion on Chart 12, is of course among those needed to complete R_2 and is found also on page 64. Conforming to the sequence developed on the Word Charts or in the primer books is not a hard and fast rule. But we have outlined this sequence in order to assist users of the material and the approach in knowing what possibilities it opens up for those students who are invited to follow it.

R_2 ends with three pages of sentences followed by five pages of continuous reading which can serve as test of mastery of the ground covered thus far. The book closes with a poem which can be counted among those texts that serve as a test.

Worksheets 1-7 are associated with R_2. They follow the pattern described in Chapter 4 and can be used in a similar way as an instrument for continuous feedback so that the teacher will know that the students are working all the time towards mastery of skills necessary to become an independent reader.

By coordinating the exercises proposed in these worksheets with the introduction in the classroom of the items met above in the charts and the book, *a systematic survey of the language as it is spoken and written* will be made possible.

All through the lessons students have been reading and writing. They have been encouraged to take initiative; to listen carefully; to watch the relationship of shape and sound; to form as many criteria as are needed; to share observations they make about the language as they hear it spoken at home, in the environment, through the media; to become curious about some of the factors that influence the sound, usage, and meaning of words and into how this affects their appearance in writing; to discover as many idiosyncracies of their language as they can, stimulated as they are by the questions put to them in lessons and through the worksheets; and to write creatively and prepare themselves for greater adventures in writing.

“R_3”

The contributions of *R_3,* the Worksheets 8-14, the remaining charts, and the Book of Stories together all make “*R_3*.” The work done up to this point through the activities described so far form the basis for a linguistic growth students deserve and are not generally offered during their early elementary school education.

In the next chapter we shall be specifically concerned with the challenges of spelling in the case of the English language. The Word Charts and the Fidel associated with the contents of *R_3*, mainly through the exercises they make possible, will provide a very thorough introduction to, and a full awareness of, the demands of spelling.

Since spelling is concerned with the imagery of written words developed through historical circumstances and since no one has yet been able to prepare a reform that could be accepted by those who decide changes in these fields, *we are faced with the teaching of English as it is written today*. This can be made into a very exciting set of challenges leading almost everybody to that level of mastery only possible when the overall challenge is understood and this understanding translated into a technology.

Part of Chapter 6 is given to the study of what is involved in the phenomenon of spelling and part to the description of the games which educate everybody towards its mastery.

Since some of these games are closely associated with what we attempt in *R3* and in the Worksheets 8-12, they could have been included in that chapter. But to avoid repetition we shall ask our readers to go now to Chapter 6 and return to this page for what belongs to this chapter and is not said in Chapter 6. Reference to the Fidel Charts and the Word Charts in the next chapter can be integrated with what follows.

* * *

Our readers know that our common sense view of reading and writing involves students in such a way that they first become aware of what is asked of them, and only then engage in activities which change the awarenesses into facilities.

As teachers, we can help most by making students aware of the challenges. Their own work will provide them with the needed facility. For example, we can show them on the Fidel that there are nine differently colored *ou* found in nine columns, or ten differently colored *ea* as part of words on the Word Charts, but in a given word we cannot make them associate a particular sound to either of these signs. Only if they themselves have carefully constructed a store of associations with signs and sounds will they feel that they are confidently on top of this particular challenge. To assist in this, our common sense tells us to present in *clusters* many words in which:

1 the same *sign* is used, but with a number of different soundings, or

2 the same sound is used but expressed through a number of unusual signs.

This forces awareness that one cannot be sure of which sound to utter by simply looking at a word, that some other involvement is required. And it alerts one that learning to spell also asks for such different involvement. Looking at words is a prerequisite of learning to spell. This means that prerequisites consist in retaining which sounds go with some forms and in deciding quickly which form is needed here and now for a certain spoken word. Therefore, these exercises recommend themselves and place students in front of the open challenge in as many ways as are needed.

This is precisely what is done in "*R3*" and through book *R3* and Worksheets 8-12. Sets of words are presented in isolation so that they exemplify all the associations required by English. Sounding these words properly in the presence of the teacher and one's classmates by looking at them printed in black — with no assistance from a sentence context — will give the opportunities to students of finding out whether they have grasped the challenge of "*R3*." If the sounds uttered for a given word are those required by tradition, then we move on to the next one. If they are not, we can investigate with the class what it could be, looking at probabilities. We may end up with two or three likely ones that sound English. The dictionary can be used as a final arbiter on whether this spoken word exists with *this* particular spelling.

But several of the words met can be used together in sentences such as those found on the odd numbered pages of *R3*. It is then that the contrast gives one's awareness some depth and shows how we organize what we retain. This retention is needed to produce confidence. So we must do what we can to secure it. The worksheets suggest exercises which are helpful in this. Others can be made part of the class lessons — in particular writing sentences which include many different words requiring the same sound for the same spelling or many different sounds of the same spelling. For example:

> the couple got in trouble in the doubles
>
> four courageous soldiers had enough courage to shoulder it
>
> pears neither wear nor tear
>
> if the weather allows, the sergeant will take his sweetheart Pearl to the theater in Seattle to a great reading of poetry.

A lesson or two spent composing such sentences with the most ambiguous signs will neither be a waste of time nor generate a sense of futility. Indeed, the exercise is so creative that it has on all occasions we know of, generated a great deal of interest in very different groups of students.

Awareness of spelling is only one of those awarenesses we can generate at the "R_3" level. Some of the other exciting ones include:

1 *Considering any one of the twenty Word Charts, can we produce sentences using only these words.*

To begin with such a challenge may appear too great. But by allowing time for it, in ten minutes or so, a first sentence will be proposed, followed at once by a number of others.

Clearly not all charts are equally difficult to penetrate in this way. Perhaps by alternating easy and demanding ones we can keep the excitement going. Because we want to stimulate creativity we should not offer our own answers but join our class and work like them on the challenge suggested. If no one can offer a first sentence, ours would serve as an opening. This game is generally found both exciting and productive.

To make beginning easier, the strict restriction of the game to words on only one chart can be modified to include one, two, or three words from other charts.

2 *Another exercise consists in making sentences selected from among the words on all 20 charts to produce a statement:*

- that expresses
    - sadness
    - irritation
    - satisfaction
    - gaiety or enjoyment, etc . . .

- that is matter of fact

- that states an obvious contradiction

- that relates to hope

- that is slanderous

- that is made
    - by an envious person
    - by a jealous person
    - by a kind person
    - by a generous person
    - by an elderly person
    - by a young child
    - by an invalid
    - to an invalid
    - by a guest
    - to a guest
    - by a host
    - to a host, etc. . .

Such exercises serve additional purposes besides the study of the language. They can be used to show how language is at the service of society; of social relations, and how it makes the study of how one can express specific climates held "between the lines" by a proper selection of words.

3 *Can one find among the words on the charts:*

- which are verbs, nouns, adjectives, etc. .
- which have meaning associated with them that are
    - very close
    - opposite
    - somehow related, etc.

- which refer to specific functions
    - such as jobs
    - such as states of being
    - such as conditions, etc.
- which have figurative meanings
- which are more precise, and which are more vague than others
- which are colloquial and which are formalwhich are general and which are specific

- which can be used alone and which can be used in pairs
- which generate many other words, which only themselves
- which are key words for expression in English and so on.

4 *Associations triggered by words or parts of words. Are these associations through the meaning or through the sounds, through the form of the word or through the root of the word, or through a life experience or an accidental connection.*

5 *How many of the words on the charts*

- do not evoke any meaning
- evoke a vague awareness
- evoke doubt about the meaning
- evoke a great deal which you could express spontaneously
- evoke a dreamlike association
- evoke insights either into life or into English etc.

6 *Making sentences of various lengths*

- one word sentences

- two word sentences and so on up to say fifteen word sentences
- a sentence as long as one can think of, say of 100 words.

7 *Since phrasing has been studied all along, is it possible using words on the charts to find a number of sentences to respond to various patterns. (The phrases are separated by dashes and the number of words in a phrase is indicated by the numerals.)*

1-1-1	1-2	2-1
1-2-3	1-3-2	2-1-3
2-3-1	3-1-2	3-2-1

Exercises 6 and 7 are connected with important awarenesses that natives have but find lost in their subconscious mastery of their spoken language. To give these exercises to the students will help them bring to the fore this reality of composition within the vocabulary one owns and thus help them in mastering writing.

In this chapter, we limited ourselves to exercises that make one who is a user of the language and already knows it in its spoken form, into a user of its written form. This we called "R_3." We shall see later how one becomes a user of the written form to acquire knowledge one does not have. We call that "R_4." R_3 is already a vast field as shown by this chapter and the next. It will be found to be a necessary component of the other numerous *R's* that we shall encounter when in Chapter 7 we survey reading in its aspects capable of being isolated. Because "R_3" is the foundation of all future development in this medium it deserves our serious attention and we suggest that the studies that are possible with the means our technology makes available, be made part of the language arts programs at the elementary school levels and remedially at the subsequent levels. "R_3" integrates "R_0," "R_1" and "R_2." Therefore "R_3" corresponds to a real level of awareness of the language and of oneself as a user of it. In fact, at "R_3" we can stop the foundation of reading and writing and put on top of it any or all the other "*R*"*s* which do not necessarily have links with each other. All have some connection with "R_3" and so "R_3" is the measure of the level of literacy implicitly sought after by so many investigators in the field of reading and now made in this book as explicit as it needs to be.

This long chapter may be found at the same time too loaded with thoughts and insufficiently illustrated with examples. Had we allowed for a sufficient number of examples it would have been much longer and unwieldy. Perhaps the explanation given here will be found adequate if readers do not limit themselves to its contents, but instead look at its suggestions while having in front of them the charts and the Fidel (mini or classroom version) as well as the books R_2 and R_3 and Worksheets 1-7 and 8-14.

A *Book of Stories* goes with "R_2" and "R_3." Questions on their literal and literary contributions form part of Worksheets 13 and 14.

Part III

Beyond "R_3"

6 Spelling

The Theory

Every one of us has a large number of opportunities, in a lifetime, to examine closely what spelling means. But not everyone takes the opportunity when it is forced upon them. So many of the people I meet who have a spelling problem do not go further than observing, "I am poor at spelling." The severest problems may require very special treatment, but most problems can be handled with relative ease once we understand what is involved in the challenge and meet it with common sense.

We devote this section to that study.

Because the word "to spell" has two meanings, we must first separate them so that confusion does not occur by shifting from one meaning to the other.

The straightforward meaning of spelling — saying the names of the letters (as assigned by the alphabet) in the order they come in the word when uttered — we shall consider as the *easy challenge* and deal with it in its right place and thoroughly. Here, we only need to say that this meaning is an adjunct of the complex challenge represented by the second meaning which will need all our attention before we can show why the first meaning is taken care of so easily.

Hence, for a while, we shall not be concerned with that meaning, and the word "spelling" will refer to the complexity we shall be studying. In order to keep the reader in contact with this request we shall represent the word "spelling" by *S* for its complex meaning and by *s* for the easy meaning. A study of what is covered by the meaning of the reality represented by *S* may require that we isolate components that we shall represent as S_1, S_2, S_3. . . . The letter *S* and its subscripts are indicators of the various realities on which we shall work.

Not all written languages are alphabetical. Not all people are seeing or hearing people. To keep these facts in mind may assist us in the study of *S*.*

Spelling will represent different challenges according to the populations we are concerned with. Working on the challenges met by the Chinese (whose language is not alphabetical), by blind people (who never saw a word), by deaf people (who never "heard" a word), may provide instruments needed to really

* A short way of expressing the realities referred to by the complex meaning of "spelling."

understand the challenges met in alphabetical languages by seeing and hearing people.

At the base of *S* we must place *perception.* Somehow this must first be made to work in order to allow some reality to exist in any mind. We shall call S_1 the component that comes from the contribution of perception to the final complex act of mastered spelling.

Immediately next to perception we must place *evocation.* This is the movement of the mind that proves to itself that something internalized is available by the process of *recall.* Recall we shall see is itself complex. We shall call S_2 the component that comes from the contribution of evocation to the final complex act of mastered spelling.

Immediately next to evocation we shall place *re-cognition*, the movement of the mind that matches the evoked recall and the original *retained* impact from perception. S_3 will be the name of the component that results from its contribution.

Re-cognition is an intellectual process. With it we must notice the presence of an affective movement which we shall call *certainty* of which *conviction* is one aspect. Certainty results from actual energy released and that follows actual matchings, while conviction results from a belief that a matching took place — which means that sometimes it may not have taken place. S_4 and S'_4 will refer to these two aspects of this component in the final product.

Perception and evocation can be separated and can be merged. When they are merged they create an entity we shall call *triggering,* whose dynamics is that one component can produce the other. Perception triggers evocation and evocation triggers perception and our mind can be aware that one and the other are present in it, together and separately.

One more component is the connection between words, looked at both as written and spoken. This we can call the *encoding-decoding* component (or S'_5 and S_5). A definite set of sounds (the spoken word) triggers a definite set of signs merged into a written word (or encoding); a definite set of signs (the written words) triggers a definite set of sounds (or decoding).

Finally, a further connection can be found in the component of *meaning* associated with words. This connection is not necessary in order to produce a correctly written word or in order to utter correctly a word when looking at it. But since for many many words, meaning is a trigger of a form, we shall include this component as S_6.

In the above hierarchy of components we have related the learner — who has to see a word in his mind before he can put it down on paper — to himself at work mentally in ways that are distinguishable by specific criteria. In perception, the criterion is that words are outside oneself, exist per se; and that they can be reached or that one can let them affect oneself. In evocation, the criterion is that one's mind has the power to use some energy available within to form an *image* that is distinctly of a word and clearly willed by oneself. In recognition, the criterion is dual:

1 that the image is truly the one wanted, and

2 that it belongs to one's mind.

Certainty is its own criterion and serves as a censor to pass the image as adequate. Conviction does the same job but is not a criterion.

These four components (perception, evocation, recognition and certainty) are the backbone of the work one has to do in order to acquire the necessary mental inventory of word images and reach the state that can be identified as that of a competent speller.

Awareness that in one's mind there are triggers specially connected with words and that they become precisely what makes encoding and decoding be what they are, gives this field its ad hoc character. When the trigger is a meaning, an association is added to the mechanisms above (encoding-decoding). The student has to discover, however, that for the complex act of spelling to take place, the presence of meaning is neither a sufficient nor a necessary condition.

S_1: Perception

S_1 would demand different things from different subjects. A deaf student who can see, will see the form as a reality and may recognize it under different lightings as remaining the same. A blind student will have an image of the word if he can touch it and learn its shape, unless he has an entry into another code (like Braille) and substitutes, for his lack of seeing a form, the tactile impact he gets from the patterns of dots.

A seeing student who knows what words are, can (like the deaf one) perceive the ad hoc form representing a particular word. Whether it is a Chinese character or a string of letters, makes little difference at this stage.

Perception is a necessary component of spelling and must be given its place. Because perception can be a conscious activity with which every one of us can have an intimate dialogue it can become stronger and stronger. We therefore know already that we shall have to involve our students in activities that make them attentive to this component. From these they will learn to create the automatic survey of words in front of them needed to know exactly what they are looking at.

S_2: Evocation

S_2 is not as immediately understandable. Indeed, each student must reach a very personal awareness that he or she can affect the retina from inside so as to give the feedback that what is sought after is being achieved.

For blind students the retina is replaced by fingertips.

To ensure that students understand what is meant by evocation, exercises must be invented which force such an awareness.

For example, if a part of a word is removed by presenting to a student the form *s t p* on a chalkboard, the gap is perceived simultaneously with the letters present. By handing out the chalk to a student we can see whether he inserts *o, e, oo,* or *ee,* all of which can come to mind. Varying this exercise will convey to the students the difference between perceiving what is there and evoking what is not there.

Later in this chapter we shall give further examples of the exercises that are functional in the education of evocation and therefore functional in making people pay attention to what will make them into better spellers.

S_3: Recognition

S_3 needs to be fortified through specific exercises in which only recognition is acted upon. Among them can be counted those mentioned above for S_2, but there are many others. For instance, spacing the letters, making them smaller, making some smaller and some bigger, shifting from lower case to capitals and conversely.

Another powerful exercise is cutting words in half longitudinally and presenting only one half to the students. In it we learn that our *imagination* and not only our images intervene in the acts of recognition. A close examination of what we do tells us that we scrutinize the given form and make a number of "visual hypotheses" rejecting, one after the other, those that do not lead to a completion of the word. Often quite suddenly we discover the details that make obvious how these designs are connected and their clear relationship to our chosen image.

Because here we are relating to words in ways that are not the requirements of reading — whose function is to serve as a vehicle for the meaning and not to stress the words per se — we force awareness of recognition and the role it plays in the actual acts of reading when we are beginners and now, when we want to master spelling. The same kind of exercises can let us penetrate more deeply into the understanding of both what is required to be a good proofreader, and how much of a word needs to be consciously perceived in the act of reading for us to move along in the scanning of a written sentence.

Recognition of a word may mean that only a certain portion of that word needs to be given to trigger its gestalt. It also may mean that some alteration within a word can be tolerated without disturbing the "perception" of the intended word. A special focusing is needed to reveal the alteration or alterations in the word which are not noted in the usual scanning that fast readers do.

S_4: Certainty

The affective component S_4 reveals itself when, in the act of reading we are struck by a word which for example, cannot be integrated with the rest of the sentence and have this still make sense. We stop, we go back, re-read, start asking questions about what we have read, and we make hypotheses about which word should be changed into which other to make this sentence understandable. We feel we *are* then present in the act in a way we normally are not. We experience that time no longer glides along smoothly as it does otherwise when we do not need to use ourselves consciously for changing words.

Once we know that affectivity is profoundly interwoven with our reading — within the act itself — we can make room for it in our study of spelling and we can distinguish S_4 from S'_4 — that is, certainty from conviction. When we have done the jobs that lead to the mastery of spelling we know ourselves as certain that what we look at is as it should be and what we put down is likewise. Certainty is affectivity without sentimentality, while conviction retains some sentimentality leading to opinions and beliefs. In the state of certainty we know absolutely — that is, without any doubt. Applied to spelling this means that we have all the necessary criteria to know that the form we conceive for any given word is in conformity with the many invisible rules which demand this form and no other for that word, in this sentence.

In a state of conviction, on the other hand, we extrapolate and we sense probabilities. We also sense perhaps, the remote possibility that all that is necessary to generate certainty in us has not been mobilized — or cannot be. For indeed, we know what activities are necessary to retain these gestalts which make written words inevitably what they are. Although they are influenced by historical accident, they display inner consistencies in their apparent capriciousness.

Because of these affective components we may have to offer our students exercises that create awareness of the difference between a superficial connection to words and a profound involvement in their retention which respects what they are.

One such exercise is a deliberate violation of verbal habits as we experience when someone says: "I have went" or "I saw you tomorrow," that betrays the emotional component in the fabric of speech in the knower when hearing these expressions.

We can offer verbal statements that are immediately recognizable as needing some modification to agree with existing habits as in the above. And then suggest others which are accompanied by doubts that disappear after some reflection and a suggestion that if matters changed here or there all would be well. For example, the use of "of" for "from" or for "for." Others can be found for which the only possibility is for doubts to persist. This is the case of those who do not have an entry into what a statement is all about or do not care how it is expressed.

Once we have found that we are all susceptible to finding ourselves sometimes in one or the other of these categories, we see that the words we meet are of three kinds:

1 those we know with certainty,

2 those about which we can for a while feel uncertain until some criterion comes to our rescue to allow a decision that the gestalt should be this and nothing else, or need specific alterations,

3 those about which we accept uncertainty and remain with it.

Learning to spell well is to enlarge the first category to include more and more of the words of the language; and concurrently, to widen one's experience so as to have access to more and more areas of living with the result of widening the meaning of words and adding more and more words to one's vocabulary to express all of one's experience.

Where the boundaries between these classes of words fall is an individual matter for each of us. These boundaries once scrutinized may lead to useful conclusions about our apprenticeship of spelling. It would be difficult to find examples that would serve all readers. In English, words that make us feel as we do when we are in the second category, can be found among those that end in *-able* or *-ible*. Whenever we feel the need to refer to a dictionary we know what is meant by the above categorization. Frequent reference indicates a shaky confidence.

Since words that refer to the third category abound in areas where "some authority" in a group decides to propagate a spelling which has no basis in etymology, sound, or common sense, we can see how people cope with them.

> For example, in "tyre" (British) there is no justification for *y* instead of *i*, in "sovereign" there is none for including *g*, and in "island" there is none for including *s*.

Other gestalts get some guidance from etymology so one does not have to count only on memory, but a look at some American spellings will reveal how "some authorities" enter the field and create problems for the apprentice.

> For example, should *neumonia* be adopted for *pneumonia* there would still remain a mystery about its spelling while we would lose the help in holding the present spelling in mind which results from the connection with an area of experience — breathing — and some insight into how technical words in English are formed by borrowing from Greek and Latin.

It is possibly a false simplification to do away altogether with unsounded letters. This narrow view, that concerns itself purely with remembering the spellings, does away with the correct basis for retention which is, in fact, a widening of experience. In the traditional orthography of English words written using the Roman alphabet, there have been many sources for the choices of spellings — some helpful and others strictly arbitrary. In the first category of sources we place the word "psychology" that tells a great deal that "sikologi" will not, and in the second we place "debt" in which the *b* has been inserted when some authority made a false connection to a Latin word that is not the direct source of that word.

The preoccupation of many people with simplification and rationalization seems to result not from a proper study of the powers involved in the act of spelling but from an idea that takes hold of its proposer and leads to suggestions which so far have not prevailed. A number of proposals for simplified and better adapted phonetic signs exist and have fascinated many for a long time. Had they been successful in the political and administrative arenas, we would have adjusted to them; but there is no guarantee even then that there would be no problem spellers in the schools. Indeed, every reform concerns itself not with the challenges of making good spellers in any language, but with an a priori view that only the *s* meaning of spelling exists, and that *S* with its complexities will be taken care of automatically by the proposed reform.

A theoretical study of the reforms still alive in the field, shows that none of the reforms is really concerned with making good spellers of all of us.

Reformers as reformers, live the affective component all the time, but they only know it in the social, political and economic areas. They do not let it penetrate their study in such a way that they can surely be concerned with the totality of the challenges of spelling (S).

S_5: Encoding-Decoding

A great deal has been written about *decoding* and *encoding* which we labeled S_5 and S'_5. In our present study we can understand their place and role better when we relate to the *triggering* of the dynamics found in perception and evocation as they are associated in the mind of each of us.

However subtle this process, it must be an *energy transaction,* and we are helped when we keep this in mind. The subtlety only adds the difficulty of being in contact with minute amounts of energy that draw far less of our attention to themselves than the not so inconsiderable amounts required in our waking life to cope with events.

Every word scanned has a physiognomy in terms of the energy expenditure required to design it on a surface. Anyone learning to draw a Chinese character not yet completely mastered will come to that conclusion. Such a conclusion, not only applies to any alphabetical language, but must be contemplated if we want to understand encoding-decoding in terms of energy.

Conscious decoding, which is needed by any reader meeting a word new to him or her, may be an important key in the making of good spellers and probably good readers and writers. And conscious decoding can be seen as a complex of acts that clearly involves energy. Staying with a word requires a certain configuration of the muscles of the eyeballs, the muscles for focusing, and the muscles of the neck to release those of the eyes so as to let them move to the next part of the word. The fact that we do all this very fast does not reduce its reality. We spend different lengths of time on:

1. the "natural" components of a word, guided by recognition, imagination, the retention of context needed to make sense, and
2. the alternate concentration and relaxation required to focus on the components.

This complex *is* the energy distribution associated with each configuration of a written word.

Decoding (or S_5) is the conscious involvement that permits the successful carrying out of such a complex activity.

Thus each word can be associated with a spectrum of energy that reflects exactly its physiognomy and which needs to be made one's own before encoding (or S'_5) can be contemplated.

To clarify this point the following exercise may be sufficient. Attempt to put down a 30 stroke Chinese character. How many times have you lifted your head and looked at the design? How many times have you stopped, to survey the activity? How many times have you gone over a stroke, already put down? Which were your doubts? When did you tell yourself the job had been done? Well done?

Fluent writers may have to do similar things, but since these are telescoped together and highly automated they seem to happen almost "instantaneously."

Conscious decoding is a specialized blending of perception, evocation, energy scanning and storing, working together. This last point is generally overlooked because we all know that we are *not* required to remember the words once the meaning is received in reading or conversation.

Thus, for a while, we must hold the sequence of the associated signs and sounds that give the word its reality (i.e. make it capable of being perceived) and which may trigger a meaning. This duration of the temporary storage is soon neglected as not deserving our attention although without its happening often reading would not make sense. For example, the relationships between the various words of the sentence which give it consistency form the gates that let us go on reading or writing the sentence. For this to be possible we must hold each word as it is and let it make its contribution to the message. As soon as either a required modification in a word to express its grammatical function (plural, tense, adverb) is not present, or one specific word (preposition, conjunction, even noun, adjective or verb) is replaced by another that blurs the meaning of the sentence, we know that we are forced to stop and read again in order to decide what is wrong.

In all this, decoding is blended with meaning to produce the right spelling when spelling is the testimony of grammatical adaptation rather than of physiognomy.

S_6: Meaning

S_6 has been encountered in the words of the last three paragraphs in one of its manifestations; that of the modification of words because some rule of speech requires it. In writing we often carelessly leave off a final *ed* in verbs requiring it to express a past tense, or a final *s* needed in the third person singular of the present. These are counted as spelling mistakes, as are missing words in a hastily written sentence. A careful re-reading would have most likely brought these omissions to the fore so they could be put right. But since they are errors specially manifested in the *writing* of words, they constitute a special category in the study of the problems of spelling.

Meaning both stops us and makes us move ahead. The first case has been considered above: it demands reconsideration of what has been done and makes us capable of correcting certain kinds of mistakes, which we all make. But when meaning makes us move ahead, its function in our becoming good spellers is counter productive. Anything that removes our watchfulness of the words per se does not assist us in becoming conscious of the shape which is something we need in order to be certain of what should be put down.

People who separate reading from writing and whose definition of reading is solely the gathering of meaning, may have created a difficulty for themselves if they later decide to concern themselves with spelling. If they are so specialized that they leave to other experts the solution of the challenge of spelling, they may be excluding themselves by their own definition of reading which does not involve individual word recognition. But if we accept that most readers are also writers, and that in that capacity they must instruct their hand to put down signs one after the other to produce words other people may want to read, then the respect of the conventions in this act, or respect for spelling, becomes important. Meaning is not enough. To transmit meaning requires correct spelling as much as correct grammar; in some respects spelling reflects grammar too!

Among the words of any language there are many to which a number of meanings have been associated. A word with one spelling and one sounding may have several meanings. In this case it is the context which must let us know at once which meaning is referred to.

Then there are other words with the same spelling but —

1 with either different soundings to convey altogether different meanings (e.g. live/live, wind/wind), or

2 with an alteration in stress so that the linguistic function of the word is altered (e.g. permit/permit) — called *homographs.*

Finally, there are words that sound the same but which are written with different spellings that make their distinction direct or their confusion detectable by the context (e.g. led/lead and strait/straight) if one knows that there is more than one spelling for the sequence of sounds in these words — called *homonyms.*

* * *

The overall problem of spelling exists because:

1 a decision was made to write down a language that was already used orally for expression and communication;

2 those who undertook the transmutation of the spoken speech into the written speech did not measure accurately the amplitude of the challenge they gave themselves; and

3 the task was undertaken by many people living at different times and having various insights into the matter or facing different vested interests.

As a result we are, in the successive generations, facing adjustments for which no one wants to take responsibility. We resort to either teaching spelling without quite knowing how, or to accepting that

1 good spelling is for the gifted (like math) while

2 the majority will never learn to spell well.

Teachers accept to be counted among the latter.

But after our study above, the situation may have changed. It seems common sense that if all the components we have found in the study of spelling do exist, we need to educate people to use themselves in such a way as to master the skills involved.

It seems common sense that we do not postpone meeting these challenges because of some preconception which may take the form of an attractive theory of reading. If we do not, this may mean that we can encounter the challenges of spelling at the beginning of our school life in the primary grades (K-2), provided we know how to do it functionally and without any pressure.

The rest of this chapter is concerned with this.

Games

The Fidel* (8 charts with columns of signs in color) is the basic reference for the study of spelling by students.

By simply looking at the Fidel, it is clear that the challenge of English spelling is considerable. We can notice that if we organize the English language in terms of all the sounds and then of all the spellings associated with each of the sounds, we find the following:

1 There are 37 basic sounds — 14 pure vowels and 23 consonants (each represented in one color only).

2 There are 9 compound vowels and 13 compound consonants (all represented in two colors).

3 In all there are 23 vowels and 36 consonants used in the ordinary language.

---

* This is an Ethiopian word used to describe such a table of signs and borrowed from that language because it was in Addis Ababa in 1957 when for the first time I did this type of analysis of the signs and sounds of the English language.
(See Appendix A, p. 295-297)

4 Only 8 of these sounds (columns) are represented by a single spelling, and these are all compound sounds. The remaining 51 sounds show by the length of their respective column that they can be transcribed with between 2 and 24 forms — with the majority requiring more than 10.

But the challenge is more circumscribed than it appears since often there may be only one or two common words in English requiring a particular spelling (for example: *colonel* and *chocolate*).

A key is available to give teachers at least one example for each of the sound-spelling connections offered on this Fidel.

Game 1

Students are asked to look at the Fidel, while the teacher points out a word — say *ill* — and then derives from this as many English words as can be formed by touching with the pointer those additional sounds needed to produce them, either before and/or after pointing to *ill:*

> pill, till, sill, mill, fill, dill, lill, will, kill, rill, bill, hill, gill, shill, chill, jill, quill

> spill, still, skill, frill; silly, hilly, chilly; miller, tiller, killer; filling, willing, chilling; pillow, willow, billow

Other words with which students can then play the same game on their own include:

at, an; it, in; on; up; old, ode, low;

ate, ace, ail, ale, aid, ade; ice etc.

Game 2

A word is selected by someone and all its signs but one are pointed out — the wall above the Fidel is touched at the point in the sequence of signs when one is omitted. The class is then asked to complete the word by suggesting alternative choices for the missing sign. In many cases there may be more than one solution to the problem. For example:

____at	yields	*pat, sat, mat, gnat,* *fat, that, cat, rat,* *hat, bat, chat*
p____t	yields	*pat, pet, pit, pot,* *put, peat, pout*
pi____	yields	(with the second sound the one in *pit) pip,* *pit, pin, pill, pith,* *pick, pig, pitch* (with the second sound the one in *pipe)* *pipe, pine, pile, pike*

This game aims mainly at educating *word imagery* and can be played with words of any length. For example:

___*t*	yields	*it, at, ought, eat, eight, oat, out*
*str*___*t*	yields	*strut, street, straight strait*
___*eceive*	yields	*receive, deceive*
*rel*___*ve*		*relieve, relive*

A large number of lessons can be devoted to this game so long as the students show that they are interested in playing it because it challenges them and is neither too easy nor too difficult.

Game 3

Write a sign on the chalkboard that is part of a limited number of words and ask students to evoke one of them and write it down, the class collects the samples and discusses correctness or error. For example:

augh may bring to mind *taught, caught, daughter, naughty, naught*

someone may suggest	*laugh, laughter, laughing, etc.* (accepted when the game allows forming this letter-combination by choosing signs from two different sound-columns.)

ea which the class can find in seven columns on the Fidel, can generate seven lists of words — the words in each list having the same sounding for this sign. A separate list may be made for words in which the two letters have two sounds like: *create, theater,* or *Seattle.* A student's paper or the chalkboard could look something like this:

e a

eat	feather	bear	learn	heart	great	pageant	theater
ear	spread	wear	early		break		
teacher	lead	pear	pearl				
lead							

ou for which there are nine soundings, can be treated likewise.

But the game is particularly useful when the spelling chosen is found in very few words and has only one or two soundings, or when it has only one or two examples for one sounding. For example:

aigh yields *straight, straighten* etc.

eye	yields	*eye, eyes, eyed, eyeing, eyeball, eyelid, eyelash, eyeglass* etc.		
eigh	yields	*height*		*sleight*
			as well as	
		eight	*weigh*	*sleigh*
		eighty	*weight*	*freight*
		eighteen	*neighbor*	etc.
		eighth	*neighborhood*	

Because there are more than 200 spellings on the Fidel that can be treated in this way, Game 3 will extend over a number of hours.

Game 4

Producing alternatives to the key provided with the Fidel. Each column has been treated in the Key. Now students are asked to find at least one word for each sign. If there is only one word for one of the spellings in a certain column students will of course propose the one on the Key even if they have not been told what it is, providing they know it.

But if there are a few possible words using a certain sign, the class together may produce some of them or all of them. When examples are not found on the Word Charts (or in *R3*) the teacher has the opportunity to introduce a possible example by illustrating the meaning.

> For example: for *sth* in the fourth consonant column saying (or pointing out) "The Panama Canal cuts through a narrow strip of land which joins Central and South America. It is called the______of Panama."

In this example, the context of the sentence may then trigger in the minds of English speakers the proper word to fill the gap.

When the class together is finding as many examples as possible for the various signs in one of the Fidel columns, the chalkboard or a student's paper might look like this:

sh *shock, shoe, splash, wish. . . . .*

ch *chef, machine, michigan, chamois. . . .*

t *action, generation, partial, pretentious. . . .*

s *sugar, sure, pension, expansion. . . .*

ss *tissue, obsession, pressure. . . .*

c *precious, appreciate, special. . . .*

sch *schist* (Br. Eng. schedule). . . .

sc *conscience, conscientious. . . .*

che *cache, moustache. . . .*

When students can use the Fidel in the ways Games 1-4 permit, applications of the acquired skill present themselves in

1 pointing out a sequence of words which form a sentence that is then read by the class

2 writing down the pointed-out sentences on paper after they have been read

or on paper immediately after they have been pointed out and then reading them from the paper

or on the chalkboard by one or a few students who have been asked not to watch the pointing-out but to write from what they hear the other students reading as they watch the pointer.

3 one student in the class dictating orally a sentence he has written by himself; another student pointing it out on the Fidel, while a third writes it directly on the chalkboard. The class then considers both productions and sees where they agree or where they need to be modified to be made correct — all of this is supervised by the teacher who may also raise questions when students do not.

Besides the games with the Fidel, there are a few other games we play to educate the powers of the mind involved in *S*. Here are a few.

Game 5

One group of games is called "Truncating Words." In such games, words are written with parts of them missing.

In one form of this game words are written with gaps to be filled with one sound (rather than one letter) when read aloud. If there is only one sign that has been cut out, we already know how to play it orally as we did with the Fidel in Game 2. But if more than one sign is cut out it is a new game. For example, can one see in *m_th_ _* a well-known word? Are there many more ways of completing this word? What are some? Or what solutions come for

ex_ _ _ _ ation? A few are:

examination	*explanation*
exaggeration	*exclamation*
	exploitation

In a second form of this game, words written clearly or typed are cut horizontally. For example, if a word such as *november* is written[*] or typed in italics and then cut with scissors into two halves, and then both halves are offered separately to people to say what word it triggers in them, it becomes possible to come into contact with $S_1 + S_2 + S_3$ in which imagination may be needed differently by the two halves.

More complex games result from mixing both types of truncations and endless examples can be produced in no time. Such games can be played as long as they yield results. They can be judged also from the demonstration of interest, or the lack of

---

[*] The size of the type will depend on whether we show the word to a class or one individual near us.

it, by the learners. Students can be asked to produce their own samples and submit it to their classmates for judgment: was it too easy? too hard? cleverly done? entertaining? does each display an understanding of the extent to which words can be mutilated and still recognized? or is the operation random and successful by chance only? etc.

These games clearly concern the articulations of evocation upon perception and therefore cannot fail to contribute to the student's education in this field. But since they also involve imagination, consciousness of what recognition is, initiative, and some sense of one's responsibility, they go beyond the scope of learning to function as a good speller.

Game 6

Another set of games basic to our common sense approach to reading and writing can be presented here because by itself it contributes a great deal to the education of the person-as-speller with which we are working in this chapter. The Game of Transformation (already met in Chapter 4) is based upon the observation that our intellect can link words in a number of ways of which "algebraic relationships" (such as addition or substitution) form one. It is an essential one because it connects with:

- the economical process chosen by the founders of spoken languages as a means of producing large vocabularies out of a limited number of sounds,

- a property of our minds which establishes associations to ease retention of intellectual matters.

By selecting only four operations (addition, insertion, substitution and reversals) we can propose a vast number of exercises which, while serving the purpose of making people into better spellers, make them also into more attentive workers capable of more concentration — into people who can have access of their inventory of words in a manner neither simplistically phonetic (*sat, mat, pat. . .*) nor through meaning (*table, surface, chart, furniture. . .*) but through contrived rules that mobilize the intellect and its powers.

Because this game appeals to a variety of mental powers (which appear somewhat different in the case of different languages in which the game has been developed) and because it appeals to people of any age beyond five, we have made it the basis for the selection of the vocabulary on the Word Charts (see Chapters 4 and 5).

Here we only need to illustrate the game:

- *at* $\xrightarrow{a}$ *pat* is an *addition*

  pat $\xrightarrow{r}$ *tap* is a *reversal*

  pat $\xrightarrow{s}$ *sat* is a *substitution*

  pat $\xrightarrow{i}$ *past* is an *insertion*

- To go from *at* to *is* we can use two different routes made of two successive operations:

  $at \xrightarrow{s} it \xrightarrow{s} is$ or $at \xrightarrow{s} as \xrightarrow{s} is$

- To go from up to stop, we can change up to pup by addition, pup to pop by substitution, pop to top by another substitution, and *top* to *stop* by addition. This can be gathered in a schema in this way:

  $\underline{up} \xrightarrow{a} pup \xrightarrow{s} pop \xrightarrow{s} top \xrightarrow{a} \underline{stop}$

  or other alternatives, such as

  $\underline{up} \xrightarrow{a} pup \xrightarrow{s} pop \xrightarrow{s} pot \xrightarrow{a} pots$

  $\xrightarrow{r} \underline{stop}$

- In some cases we need to add to the above transformations what we may call "equivalences" in order to allow some other interesting or clever series of associations.

  There are two kinds of equivalences:

  1 we accept as equivalent all sounds assigned by the language to a given sign (11 for *a,* 11 for *u,* 12 for *o,* 7 for *ea,* 9 for *ou* etc. . .) and we do not count as a transformation the shift from one sounding to another sounding in that sign in the next word. For example:

  $are \xrightarrow{a} fare$ the change in the sound of *a* is not counted; only the addition of *f*

Since all the soundings of a sign are found looking across the columns of the Fidel, this is called "horizontal" equivalence.

2 we accept as equivalent all the different spellings of a sound. For example in *fun* $\xrightarrow{s}$ *phone* the change in spelling in both the beginning and ending consonants sounds is not counted since the same sound is maintained; only the substitution in the middle.

Since all those spellings for one sound appear in the same column on the Fidel this is called "vertical" equivalence.

Now to go from *up* to *stop* using equivalences we can have (note: **h** for horizontal and **v** for vertical are used here to make the equivalences clear to teachers. We are not proposing that the students label these unless it intrigues them):

h

up $\xrightarrow{s}$ *us* $\xrightarrow{s}$ *is* $\xrightarrow{s}$ *it* $\xrightarrow{a}$ *pit* $\xrightarrow{r}$ *tip*

pit $\downarrow s$ *pot*; *tip* $\downarrow s$ *top*

pot $\xrightarrow{r}$ *top*

v

up $\xrightarrow{a}$ *pup* $\xrightarrow{s}$ *putt* $\xrightarrow{s}$ *pot* $\xrightarrow{a}$ *pots* $\xrightarrow{r}$ *stop*

other examples:

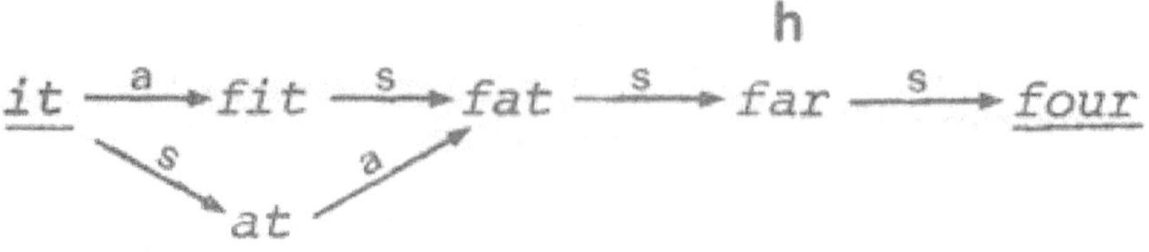

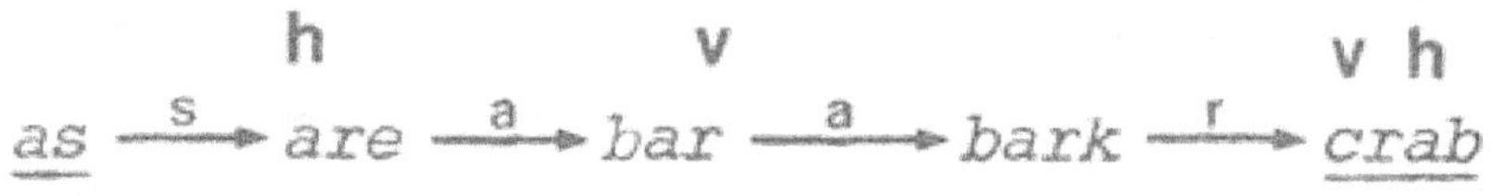

h v v h

as —s→ are —a→ bar —a→ bark —r→ crab

- Some transformations are curious because of the meanings we associate with the words: For example:

hot to *cold;* *light* to *dark;* *solid* to *liquid*

and

soft to *hard;* *fat* to *thin*

bad to *good;* *war* to *peace*

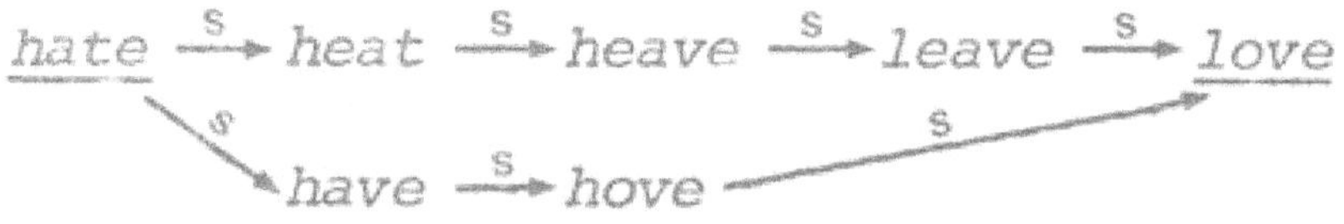

hate —s→ heat —s→ heave —s→ leave —s→ love

hate —s→ have —s→ hove —s→ love

or the converse, since the number of sounds in the first word is the same as the second (see point 7 (1) below)

- Some other transformations reveal peculiarities of English. For example:

up →a *pup* →s *sup* →r *pus* →s *fuss* →s *fun* →a *funny* →r *enough*

up →s *us* →a *pus*

where 6 vertical equivalences have been used.

- Some challenges are beyond the rules of the game and thus unfeasible:

  1 Since subtraction is not counted among the operations, the starting word cannot have more sounds than the final word.

  2 Since we can only add one sound or compound sound there are numerous situations in which we need simultaneously two separate sounds to complete the transformation and this makes the sequence impossible. For example, in going from *up* to *unless* we need "un" (two separate sounds) to finish the job once we arrive at *less*. Neither *uless* or *nless* are English words. And *one of the rules of the game is that all intermediary words must make sense for English-speaking players.*

The Game of Transformation, when started early in schools, will make a big difference on how students relate to the challenges of spelling. Indeed, being aware of how words look, how sounds relate to written forms, how associations of words occur in one's mind, and how resourceful we all are, can be considered a very solid basis for the mastery of the shapes of English words.

Other Games

There are other exercises or games that can assist students in the task of mastering spelling. Here are a few:

1 Using the Word Charts — or a chalkboard on which several words have been collected while working with the Fidel — the teacher covers up a given word and asks the students to tell which it is. If the location serves as a trigger to which it is, then we only know that students can say what they think it is. But if they cannot answer, a very swift uncovering movement of the hand to let the word appear for a fraction of a second may tell us something about how much stimulus these students need in order to recall a word from the storing place in their mind. This game is usually enjoyed by students of any age and thus must have some function in the way we retain word forms. A second stage may be added to this game by asking students:

to shut their eyes and see the covered word in their mind,

then to write it with pencil on paper (or with their finger on the desk or the palm of their hand),

then for one of them to put on the chalkboard what he has put on his paper (or on the desk or his palm),

and, now for all to compare what has just been written on the board with what is on the various papers (desks or palms), and finally, if needed, with what is still covered.

A variation on the latter game is possible when the collection of words happens to be on a chalkboard, since one of them can very quickly be erased and students asked to consult their mental image to see if it is good enough for them to volunteer to write the word back in the space where it once was: the other students watching to decide whether it agrees with their mental image.

2 Distorting words by handwriting them, as so many of us do for ourselves in our personal notes (or writing them in reverse, mirror-like — as DaVinci did — or upside down), then inquiring about how we determine what word it is with some likelihood of being right.

   This exercise tells us something about our powers of recognition as well as to how we can use our intelligence in the field of spelling, and sometimes our imagination.

3 Looking at a word clearly written and finding as many written words as we can see in it. This well-known game is not of our invention but we use it after all the others to stimulate the "insight" of students and to make them relate to words with a lightness of sight that permits new words to emerge from the same source. There are words that allow a very small crop and other huge ones. For example, "blurb" produces *rub, blur,* while "potato" yields *a, at, to, too, pot, top, tot, tattoo, pat, tap, tat,* etc. and of course a word like "washington" yields more than 100 words. These examples make it evident that in this game we look at letters not sounds nor signs. That is why we put it at the end. A version of it can be tried with the restriction, that makes it much harder, of either

maintaining the sounds or the signs (or both) that they have in the original word. For example:

eigh t ee n

If the restriction of maintaining all the *signs* is followed, only these words are allowed:

eight, tee, teen, neigh

If the restriction of only maintaining *sound* is followed, these words can be added to the first list:

ate, eighty, tea, eat, neat, knee

If the restriction is the usual one of only the *individual letters,* all these can be added to the first list:

get, hit, hen, ten, net, tin, gin, night, nigh, gene. . . . .

And Now *S*

Let us now turn to *s* for a minute.

To perform *s* properly all that is required is that:

1 we examine all the signs to which we assign the 59 sounds of English (already displayed on the Fidel) and analyze them in a *new* way, but one which coincides with the *old* alphabet or set of *letters,*

2 once we have found the 26 units of the alphabet and ordered them in the traditional manner, then we give them their traditional names

3 now we can look at any word and name the letters in order from the left to the right (using names agreed on in the preceding point).

The result is a new code for each word called its "spelling" — or *s*. For example: *taught,* which is composed of two sounds (one for the two *t's* and one for the *augh)* is now "spelled" by saying "tea - aye - you - gee - aitch - tea."

A few exercises will establish these habits for the students and *s* is no longer a problem.

Now we can find an additional way to force awareness of holding the image of whole words in one's mind (which we worked on in earlier games) by playing this traditional game of *s* "backwards" and realizing it is impossible to do it without consciously consulting one's mental image of the whole word.

7 The Various Meanings of Reading

As part of our way of working with students, we found the need to distinguish components of reading we called "R_o" *the discipline of reading,* "R_1" *the reality of the spoken and written languages,* "R_2" *surveying all the sounds of English,* and "R_3" *mastering how to write all one can say.*

Until we came to "R_4," there was clearly a hierarchy formed by "R_o" to "R_3" which made it efficient to gain mastery in one "*R*" before entering extensively into the next one. Now on this foundation all the other meanings of reading "R_4". . . . . "R_n" stand side by side. There is no longer a hierarchical relationship since any one of them can be entered into at any time following "R_3." Because it forms such an important part of school life, the whole of Chapter 8 is given to seeing how the bridge between one's experience and that of others can systematically be produced. We call it "R_4."

Now in this chapter we undertake another study: we shall look at what we do with a written text when we want to relate to it in the manner demanded by the specific purposes of the reading. It is remarkable that each of us can indeed find that reading has so many different purposes by simply becoming aware of what one is doing with oneself when confronting a text, whether it was written by ourselves or by someone else. This study will present "R_5" to "R_{17}" in summary form.

"R_5"

If I were a professional *proofreader* in a printing firm or composition room, or even at an office preparing copy for an outside printer or looking over proofs returned by a printer for approval, I would have to "read" the text in a very special way which we shall call "R_5."

In this type of reading, I do not look at each paragraph to see if I get the meaning intended, but I look at the words in a manner required to make sure:

1 that no word has been put down that was not spoken by the author — out loud while recorded by someone else or to himself while writing what he wanted to "say" — whether that author is myself or someone else;

2 that every word is correctly spelled, and

3 that various grammatical rules have been observed in the writing — for example, in the order of words in each sentence, in the agreement necessitated by the use of plurals, in the agreement required by the person and tense of the verbs, and so forth.

I do not look at each paragraph to see if I get the meaning right but I look at the words in the manner required by all these prerequisites.

It is well-known that many writers are poor proofreaders of their own work, because this job requires a special relation to the text that leaves out every one of the qualities which link the act of reading to the transmission of certain information or to communication. "R_5" is an approach to texts not required of everyone although everyone uses some aspect of it to control what goes on paper when one writes a note, or letter, or a book.

"R_6"

If I were a *professional editor* at a publishing firm and was given a book to work on in order to polish it and give it a form acceptable to the author as well as one which satisfies some requirements imposed by a number of social, professional, ethical, linguistic and other considerations, I would have to read the text very differently from the reader of the published work. As editor, I have to be sensitive not only to what the author wants to say but also to whether he says it in a manner that could be called "the best way." I will weigh each word in each sentence to see whether it makes its contribution, and eliminates the generation of ambiguities, doubts and confusions. I will watch:

1 each turn of a sentence to see whether it is the most elegant and the least cumbersome possible,

2 each paragraph, to see that it "holds" together,

3 each page, to find it is justified in the flow of the story told,

4 each section, to be sure that it has the right place in the whole,

5 each chapter, to see what is its contribution to the whole work,

6 the whole work, to find out whether it has been given the greatest chance to produce the effect anticipated by the author,

7 each reference, to a supporting point made explicitly or implicitly in order to ensure that it is brought to the fore,

8 that consistency is maintained when required and that jolts for the reader are avoided,

9 that the clarity and flow of words are such that what the author wants for the public from his work is done best.

Clearly, when we read books that are edited, we do not know that besides the author, one or more people read it in the above manner. Their reading is a specialized reading, paying attention to what on the whole is better not brought to the ordinary reader's attention. The job of editors is to eliminate any trace of their participation in the work. Because it is a specialized way of reading, sometimes editors feel that their "improvements" are more important to the success of that work than is the author's contribution. Be this as it may, for our present purpose, we need only say that there may be a number of components in "R_6" according to how much is asked of an editor to put a written work in its "best" form:

> "R_6" editing for grammar of a foreigner using a language he has not mastered,
>
> "R_6" editing the work so it is uniformly clear,
>
> "R_6" recasting a work to give it a form most suitable to the audience toward which the work is aimed etc . . .

Since there are thousands of publishing firms, there are tens of thousands of readers who are aware of those just outlined relationships to written texts. This justifies underscoring the existence of "R_6."

"R_7"

If I were a *linguist* in my own language, I would pay attention to many items in a book I was reading which are not present for ordinary readers whose concern is only the content. I would be struck by sayings and would want to know where they come from. I would see forms that would be ambiguous in themselves but for some reason lost their ambiguity in the context and want to reflect on that event. I would ponder on what is context and what is it that creates it — the reader or the text? I would be struck by the blending, generally, harmoniously, of a number of languages that historically affected that language. I would ask myself whether I know the source of the words in this or that or that sentence, and marvel at the creators of new forms in languages and at their achievement in making them acceptable to so many.

A text that purports to do a particular job (entertain, inspire, inform, etc.) becomes a totally different object when read with the sensitivity of a linguist. It is looked upon in such a very different way and with instruments not suspected as being needed by the writers. Reading in this way may be concomitant with reading the work for the purpose it was written. To read as a linguist one adds "R_7" to all the "*R*"s required by the nature of the passage. "R_7" — as "R_6" is a complex of ways of reading which we can subdivide for analysis:

> "R_7" for those looking at the intricacies of protolanguages now merged together,
>
> "R_7" for those looking for special treasures in the language of the writer,
>
> "R_7" for those looking for how words trigger meanings and images, and to what extent this writer is a master of the art,

"R_7" for those looking for "the spirit" of the language, etc . . .

Linguists are in these ways specialized readers, along with being ordinary readers. They are therefore entitled to their special way of looking at material that carries meanings for every reader so that they may ascertain whether or not the work done on the language by the writer does indeed produce the desired effects.

"R_8"

If I were an *historian* wanting to know from the printed material of a certain period what people engaged in during that period, I would have to read searchingly for those details that contribute to ascertaining that what I am led to believe is grounded in fact. I would want to find in the words used by the writers of that time some relationships to a variety of components such as work, play, entertainment, religious activities, trade, commerce and industry, education and schooling, agriculture and farming, and city life — its amenities, its furniture, its eating and cooking habits, vestments, household arts, and so on.

As an historian I would read more than what is "in between the lines," although I find there is evidence for my conclusions. If I gave myself a problem — such as, how did men treat women or what did men think of women during that period? — the words they utter would document a certain view suggested in the first place by some scene or some reflection read about in some text. As an historian, I read with an eye on the descriptions of events, the quantitative aspects of life, the formulae that indicate social structures, etiquette, the world accepted as perceived and respected as an eternal reality, the grumblings of the rebellious, the dissident opinions, the preparation for social and economic or political days, the various interests revealed by the characters, the various types of moral fiber they exhibit, and so on. I would read to retain in order to document my own work, rather than to demonstrate my acquisition of knowledge as one does in "R_4."

As an historian I am sensitive to the background of the stories as much as to their content. I try to make sense today of what no longer obtains and to feel that I am on safe grounds — that is, not inventing what comes to me but rather finding that my conclusions are legitimate and will seem so to others.

Reading as an historian is a specialized way of reading that one improves upon by reading more and more in this way texts never intended as historical records. Here too, there are many subdivisions if we use content as a criterion. But there is only one way of reading if we hold all the aspects detailed above in one whole and say that "R_8" is this reading of texts that leaves in the readers a vivid sense of how people used to live in various places and under various conditions, while it opens the way to understanding their actions (collective and individual) on the basis of how *they* interpreted their actual situation and conditions.

"R_9"

If I were a *psychologist,* besides reading for other reasons, I would read to find out how the writer as a person is revealed in his writing. I would attempt to catch his outlook on life, his readiness to share himself with his readers, his motives for writing, what style he adopted and for what reasons, the extent to which the style is the man (as Buffon suggested), the selection of topics to affect his readers, the nature of his styles and his reasons for adopting it, the way in which he selects topics to affect his readers, and the way in which these topics are presented — in some cases explicitly and in others implicitly.

Besides reading every book to find out these things about the writer, I would read many books to reach an understanding of the tenets of a particular group's psychology over a given period — from one year to one generation, or even longer — in order to penetrate the taboos, the permissiveness, and the main challenges faced in the minds of the reading public of that period. Non-psychological studies such as discovering which books remained popular and best sellers while the popularity of others collapsed, would assist me in coming to an understanding of that period.

Clearly, "R_9" also has several subdivisions, covering the way of reading appropriate for social-psychologists, and several others. When compatible with the other "*R*"s, this "*R*" adds the bias present in the minds of such readers because of their specialty.

"R_{10}"

If I were a *grammarian,* I would read a particular work to find out its contribution to the expansion or the deterioration of the language, and to detect the changes it makes in the language and to discover their origins. I would be watchful of interferences by various slangs, dialects, and other cultural influences such as the effect of changes in culture upon the living language, how much strain it can stand, and how it keeps its original strength in the face of such pressures.

"R_{10}" is a specialized reading like the ones above but it can be extended further because teachers of English on the whole have been sensitized through their university courses to the qualities of the language that needs preserving. This results, at their own schools, in their acting as watchdogs that transmit to the next generation a language which serves as a vehicle for the culture, and which is capable of maintaining continuity with the many past generations.

"$\mathbf{R_{11}}$"

The vast majority of buyers of books, magazines and newspapers do their reading for reasons other than what has been discussed. Mainly, they *read for pleasure* — for fun — and this kind of reading, although special, becomes also universal.

In "R_{11}" there are no rules. It is not necessary for the text to yield information which needs, for any reason, to be retained by anyone. Its contents can be anything, and no one will be examined about them. The only guidelines are those imposed by writers who must hold their readers' attention sufficiently well that they continue reading and feel gratified by doing so.

Here the story has to generate the sense of curiosity in the readers to find out what happens — in terms of everyday life and experience — to the people the author invents or brings together. In order to hold one's interest, a text must have distinct qualities (which we shall consider in the chapters on writing) but the readers do not have to be aware of them unless they are literary critics. In fact, the less they are aware of them, the greater is their involvement in the story and their capacity to relate to the characters.

"R_{11}" is best exemplified when applied to a detective story of quality or an adventure story in which the reader is left to guess — and to almost believe that the data presented allow him to reach a conclusion long before the end of the story. Generally we as readers are wrong. If the story is well-constructed, since the author, knowing what is going to happen, selects the material and the order in which it is included in the chapters, it is possible to fool everyone.

Once a book is read, it may leave no track behind in the reader's mind. This can be considered a characteristic of "R_{11}." The pleasure is associated with the momentary states of being of the readers who feel excited, curious, and involved — and go on with their reading or gladly return to it. When "R_{11}" is associated with another "*R*" whose function includes retention, only then we notice that the memory of the readers perpetuates what struck them and we feel that "R_{11}" leaves tracks.

"R_{12}"

The nature of many memory tracks left from reading is one which plays a particularly important role in our lives. Humans have to learn a great deal in order to function in their lives. Most of this learning involves the soma, as in developing biological functions, and in this no one can learn for anyone else. But besides this direct learning, fortunately there exists another learning which can be called *learning by proxy*. This involves humans in such a manner that, while one person goes through the direct experience another, by watching or by hearing about it, goes "virtually" through a similar experience. Virtuality has its own reality and humans have made the most of it — creating through it languages, mathematics, the sciences and the arts. In this way, one generation can avoid going through the same kind of investigations carried out by previous generations. They can learn by proxy through spoken and written language (and now also through film) why some experiments did not work. Because this is an important way of learning, it was adopted spontaneously a long time ago and reading for that purpose can be found in all cultures that have developed writing. So many books that relate first hand experiences have become sources of inspiration for their readers who find that *they* do not have to explore the North Pole, or open up the Amazon, or fly over mountains for the first time in history, and so forth, in order to feel the thrill, the suspense, and the dangers mentioned by the writers.

Love stories clearly serve this function with adolescents. Psychological novels enable the general public to entertain some mental conditions which exist in everyone but are taken to extremes only by some individuals. The cathartic effect of this virtual contact with some of these enlarged experiences is one of the benefits valued by readers of these novels.

Learning by proxy would cover in fact some distinctly different ways of reading which we lump together under "R_{12}." Within "R_{12}" we find reading which leads us to commit to memory anecdotes which strike us as remarkable because of their capacity to suggest inner movements we think we need in order to "live better," but which have not come our way directly.

Also within "R_{12}" we find the reading which results in increased experience that does not express itself through any retention of any statement. This is the case in particular when people read a huge number of books of one kind: love stories, spy stories, crime stories, war propaganda stories, and so on. The material described in these books effects one's imagery, one's imagination, one's recognition. Such experiences are part of a class of experiences that can go on and on expanding and make us know it as others do: as others live it, crime as others commit it, war as others suffer under it, and so on. We may integrate into ourself all this experience by simply becoming more sensitive, more alert, more compassionate and more vulnerable to the complexity of human lives, of circumstances, of the human mind, and of mental sanity, and so forth.

"R_{12}" as much as "R_4" is one of the reasons people offer for making everyone literate.

"R_{13}"

There are people who read some books for the special purpose of finding for themselves subject matter for *meditation*. This is common among religious people who find in their sacred texts and their prayer books a source of inspiration to keep them moving on some demanding path, or to return to it. In this kind of reading labeled "R_{13}," the rules for reading other texts are, so to say, suspended. One can choose one word or a few words to focus one's mind on, until one feels that the required "spiritual work" has been done. There are no rules in "R_{13}." Individuals use their connection to the text in a very personal manner, which does not even need to be one and the same for each person. According to the state of being at the moment, such word or words may have different echoes and repercussions. Sometimes the same word suddenly gains a dimension it did not seem to have until now, although met and uttered a number of times before.

"R_{13}" does not seem to require any one of the previous "*R*"s, since fluency in reading is not a prerequisite. One seems to act as if one is hearing someone tell something to oneself and then stops listening after this has been heard. The engrossment presupposed in "R_{13}" is so particular to this kind of reading that it is not found in any other. Comprehension here is not of the content of the text but of oneself and the universe this opens — a very personal matter indeed.

"R_{14}" to "R_{17}"

Although we have already distinguished thirteen aspects of reading there are more. In this section we shall briefly review a few more.

The way of reading of profound texts subdivides into: reading *for edification* "R_{14};" reading *for intellectual growth* "R_{15};" reading for the widening of one's *perception of reality* "R_{16};" and reading *for contact with the greatest minds* "R_{17}." They can intermingle and produce again singular meanings of reading which could be given their own place in the series of "*R*"s.

Reading *The Republic of Plato* may call in all of the above "*R*"s since it does not refer to an existing state but raises what is conceived of as "eternal" matters that people must entertain in order to experience the inner education which allows one to face adequately large human issues met in government and society.

Reading the works of the mystics asks for a propensity both

1 to give oneself to such areas of experience as are known to the mystic, and

2 to let the components of these areas — developed by the reading and now part of the reader's knowledge — trigger inner movements in the readers which confirm their own mysticism.

If one is to read very specialized texts — such as metaphysical treatises, summa theologica, and texts on logic — it demands qualities of the mind already somewhat usable before one would embark upon these writings. Reading further in them will systematically educate readers to do better and better the jobs of reading concerned with widening one's perception of reality "R_{16}," thus opening for them demanding areas of enquiry.

For observant readers, writers of a certain depth are always recognizable in every one of their statements. In our study of writing we shall see why this is possible in so many cases. Great men and women not only place their stamp on the questions they raise and consider, but also upon the languages they use to express what they found.

* * *

It is clear that the examination of the various involvements of readers in texts which cover so many different inner climates and states, must be considered as having made our relationship to reading both a more complex as well as more shaded and realistic. Although elementary school teachers focus on "R_3" and all teachers everywhere on "R_4," the reality of the act of reading, which involves a large fraction of mankind, suggests that rather than being a single activity of the mind, it is a universe of experience which requires a great deal from us in order to be described adequately. In this chapter again, we have adopted the common sense attitude followed throughout this book and found that it does not do any good to be vague about the meaning of *reading* and to imagine that this word will not create confusions. It needed to be better defined as we have attempted in this chapter.

Reading is no doubt still far more complex than we have found in this chapter. We did not say a word about the incantation that accompanies the reading of poetry, for example, and about what kind of reading is involved here.

We said nothing about the reading of music, Braille, or sign languages, which many will consider outside the problems of this book while others may think this is a serious omission.

Anyone who has anything to do with reading in a serious way will find perhaps that this chapter is merely a first and elementary statement of the real complexity of this enormous field of study.

8 "R_4"

"*R_4*" is the type of reading needed for acquiring knowledge through the printed medium. It is the level of reading competence required of their students by traditional schools and colleges.

There are essentially two problems concerning "*R_4*." The first focuses upon *how new knowledge is acquired* and the second on *how to make readers improve their intake* in the areas where they want to graduate or make a living through the study of texts.

As to the first, let us note that already "*R_3*" can be a source of information presented by the written medium. If we undergo a new experience and can manage to verbalize it so that we make it available to others through our writing; if the vocabulary we use is not specialized — except perhaps when we use labels we qualify as the names of places or of people — anyone reading our letter or our article will be remaining within "*R_3*" and still find that new knowledge has reached one. A great deal of knowledge is acquired through "R_3" although it may not be useful to pass exams in the area where the learning by proxy took place.

Reading the above paragraph for instance would belong to "R_3" rather than "R_4."

Every letter we receive and read may include information we find ourselves retaining but which we shall not count as belonging to the kind of reading that goes to make "R_4."

We can see the metamorphosis of "R_3" into "R_4" in a text made of a succession of definitions ending up with a statement which everyone would call *new knowledge* and therefore belongs to "R_4" by definition although at every stage only "R_3" was being used. A definition serves as a turning point between what we already know and what is new. If retaining any definition belongs to "R_3" — because a definition is a statement in which all words but one are triggers of meaning and that single word gains its own meaning by association to all the others in that statement — a reader may clearly use "R_3" a succession of times, and yet at the end be able to assert: "I know this or that which belongs to a field of science."

Let us look for examples at the following sequence of definitions:

> Join two points *A* and *B* on a sheet of paper using a ruler. If the line thus drawn goes only from *A* to *B* (or from *B* to *A*), *A* and *B* are called its *ends* and that part of the line between A and *B*, is called a *line segment*, written *AB*.

If two segments *AB* and *BC* have one end in common (here *B*) they are said to form a *two-segment train.*

A train can have more than two segments. Four points *A, B, C, D,* can generate several trains: *ABCD* is another way of telling which of the trains has been generated (which is clearly different from say, one described by *ACDB).*

A train in which the ends are distinct is called an *open* train. Otherwise it is said to be a *closed* figure.

The segments of a closed train are called the *sides* of that figure and that closed figure is also called a *polygon.*

The simplest polygon must have 3 sides. It is called a *triangle.*

If the 3 sides of a triangle are unequal, it is called *scalene.* If two are equal, it is called *isosceles* and if all 3 are equal, *equilateral.*

We could go on like this and show that only "R_3" has been used in each of the definitions. But because the statements are definitions they generate *new* mental material. If it is retained, then "R_3" has produced new knowledge and the further verbal manipulation of this knowledge may produce further new knowledge. At that stage "R_3" will be said to have been integrated into "R_4," which clearly involves polarized attention towards mental matter not spontaneously produced by the mind of the reader and requiring a special retention — called memorization by school people.

Hence one of the attributes of "R_4" is that it asks for memorization of the statements read. In schools, tests are offered to make sure that that special retention remains operative. This, of course is not necessary in "R_3." *Acquisition of knowledge* results from "R_4" only because we say that "knowledge plus retention is the definition of 'acquisition.' " "R_3" can also leave tracks in our memory, but it is conventional not to count these memory tracks as acquired knowledge when we are not asked to restate them specifically as they were first written.

If we read "the earth is round," ("R_3") the statement becomes knowledge ("R_4") if it is remembered forever. This is true even if this knowledge has become a *perceptible* experience for humanity only during the past few years.* Even though it is "R_4," this statement is not a definition any more than "Yolanda is thin" or "Marie is young" or "the weather is cold." In each of these statements two known entities are associated in such a way as to produce an awareness of something true for the time being, but not necessarily forever. The possibility of change is not allowed in true definitions.

---

* It was known as true but not perceptible until the astronauts transmitted back to our television screens photographs of the whole earth from the distance of outer space.

On the boundary between "R_3" and "R_4" we learn to relate in both to the differences in our ways of functioning. It seems that by a certain deliberate move of our mind we affect "R_3" so as to display in it properties which were allowed previously to go unnoticed. Becoming aware of these makes "R_4" into a separate entity — one which we may now talk about and study further.

This we shall do in stages.

Generally speaking, we need to integrate with all the components we put together to make "R_3" one new mental component which gives each word we are looking at a less fleeting quality and that enables us to retain it more easily. This additional mental energy we called an *ogden.*[*] It is the energy which substitutes for the short-term memory needed in "R_3" — which holds on to words until the meaning of statements reveals itself — a long-term memory needed to keep what has been offered verbally in one's mind forever.

It requires a slightly different *presence* in the act of reading for ogdens to be associated with what one reads. Call it attention or scrutiny or watchfulness, it certainly imposes a different use of oneself as one's eyes scan the lines of a text. A kind of "mental shovel" that picks up each word and puts it in a preselected place where the mind can go and find it again where it is associated with other words and also functionally connected to the backdrops made of images, associations and to lightings which can be triggered simultaneously. The energy of the ogden spent

---

* cf. *The Common Sense of Teaching Foreign Languages* (1976) p.9

for this retention serves to "glue" the word or statement in one's mind so that it is no longer experienced as something fleeting which is permitted to vanish, but rather as a dynamic link to one's broader experience.

For one to be in "R_4" — or for "R_4" to work — means that the reading we are doing at the moment connects with our store of ogdens in such a way that they can be used as soon as needed and with such concentration, attention, initiative, and intelligence as take care of making the lightings meaningful.

In summary, "R_4," can be described as "intelligent reading." Instead of only receiving the meaning ordinarily carried by the words as happens in "R_3," in "R_4" additional meaning is squeezed from the words by appropriate means varying with the field of study.

From this we can see that "R_4" will probably require different ways of using oneself when contemplating the acquisition of knowledge in the fields of mathematics, physics, chemistry, biology; the taxonomic sciences of geology, botany, and zoology; the applied sciences of engineering, agriculture, medicine, and so forth.

Indeed, each of these specialized studies does make specific and unique demands on our minds. Memorization, although the grossest of the common factors, is considered in schools as *the* one to assist students in the acquisition of that knowledge which can later be tested by instruments which have been collectively developed. Nearly fifty years of helping remedial cases in overcoming their failure (mainly connected with an inability to remember subject matter) have taught me which techniques will lead to success. This forms a body of pedagogy for "R_4" which is surveyed here in order to see how it can generate more and more acquisition of knowledge. It is too vast to be summarized but it can be usefully illustrated on a certain number of experiences under the headings of:

> "R_4" in some mathematics lessons — geometry & algebra
>
> "R_4" in social studies — history, geography & economics
>
> "R_4" in the natural sciences — physics, chemistry & biology.

"R_4" In Some Math Lessons

Mathematical statements can become as good carriers of meaning as are everyday life statements. Like these, they trigger images that convey meaning. The everyday phrase "a butterfly on a rose" requires that the words "butterfly" and "rose" evoke specific images which are compatible with other unspecified properties such as size, color, position in space, and so on. But the words "a" and "on" must do the same so that the images are of a *single* butterfly and a *single* rose, the first connecting in space with the second in a very precise way.

Geometry

Similarly, the mathematical statement: "The medians of a triangle are concurrent and meet at one-third of the lengths from their ends on the sides of the triangle (or at two-thirds from the vertices of the triangle)" becomes understandable (if not yet proved true) if –

1. the word "median" evokes a specific line which joins a vertex of a triangle to the mid-point on the opposite side;
2. the word "concurrent" triggers the image of the third median also passing through the point where the other two medians meet;
3. the term "one-third" (or "two-thirds") suggests that the two pieces generated on each median by the point where they meet are such that one is twice as long as the other.

Since it is not certain that the statement a, b, c above can be comprehended through "R_3" alone we suggest that a diagram be drawn by the reader while verbalizing all that is done, seen, and noticed on reflection upon one's actions. Written down it would require a lot of space and we must avoid it, instead like a wordless cartoon going from left to right the reader can add the dialogue for himself and see whether this elementary geometry theorem — whose retention would make the reading belong to "R_4" — can be obtained through perceptual support which is part of "R_3."

Note that we are not concerned with the truth of the said theorem (which belongs to a mathematics lesson) but with a study of how "R_4" is linked to "R_3" on one mathematical example. It is part of "R_3" to let words trigger images so long as the material connects with one's experience. The sequence of drawings below can do precisely that, provided the words: *triangle, midpoints of sides, medians, intersect, concurrent* are labels corresponding uniquely with one of the successive drawings.

Only ⑤ may present a problem because we assume a not too obvious but correct equivalence when we shift from "one third" of the whole to one segment in each median which is "one half" of the other segment.

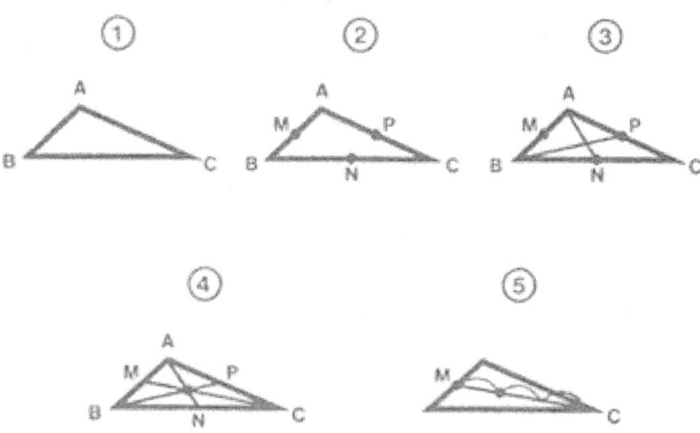

The main lesson of this elementary discussion is this. The understanding of the statement comes from its belonging to "R_4." This is done by reducing it to previous experiences by means of procedures that make it belong to "R_3" – such as a sequence of drawings — and then transmuting these into an awareness of something *new* now present in one's mind which appears as natural and as the merging and telescoping of separate but unnecessary steps provided by perceptual elements. One can now say that the level of reading is "R_4" because one can say that the words of the theorem describe what one recognizes as a *new* experience in the same way as is required when one is reporting something new in one's own experience.

Algebra

In the mathematical challenge — "Which is bigger: the square of a sum or the sum of the squares?" — the words in the question may not necessarily trigger any of the correct images for the challenge, but yet they may be part of one's vocabulary since there are locations in towns called squares and not streets and "sum" may convey from one's school days "things added together."

Since it is put as a question, one does not see what knowledge one is supposed to acquire, and so "R_4" has not yet come in. The first three words clearly are at once understandable and so can be skipped over as happens in all "R_3." But the rest can be puzzling.

There are at least two ways in which the "mysterious" groups of words are linked in a definite manner — "square of a sum" and "sum of squares" — and thus keep all the work at the "R_3" level:

1 Choose two numbers at random. Add them up. That produces *their sum.* Squaring numbers

means multiplying them by themselves (a definition which can be made part of "R_3" as we did at the beginning of this chapter). If we use this definition we can generate a succession of steps as follows:

a and b are two numbers

$a + b$ is their sum

a^2 and b^2 are their squares

$(a+b) \times (a+b)$ *or* $(a+b)^2$ is the square of their sum

$a^2 + b^2$ is the sum of the squares

The mathematical problem consists in comparing $a^2 + b^2$ and $(a+b)^2$ and deciding which is bigger. This is done in algebra courses. And it can be tested on *one* example:

2 and 3 are the two chosen numbers

$2 + 3 = 5$ is their sum

$2^2 = 4$ and $3^2 = 9$ are the squares of those two numbers

$(2 + 3)^2 = 5^2 = 25$ is the square of their sum

$2^2 + 3^2 = 4 + 9 = 13$ is the sum of the squares

and clearly the square of the sum (in this case) is bigger than the sum of the squares. Knowing that it is always the case may require other means than the verification above.

2 Choose two lengths a and b at random, and put them end to end to produce the length $a + b$. Then construct three geometric figures defined as three squares whose sides are respectively a, b, $a + b$, as in the figures below:

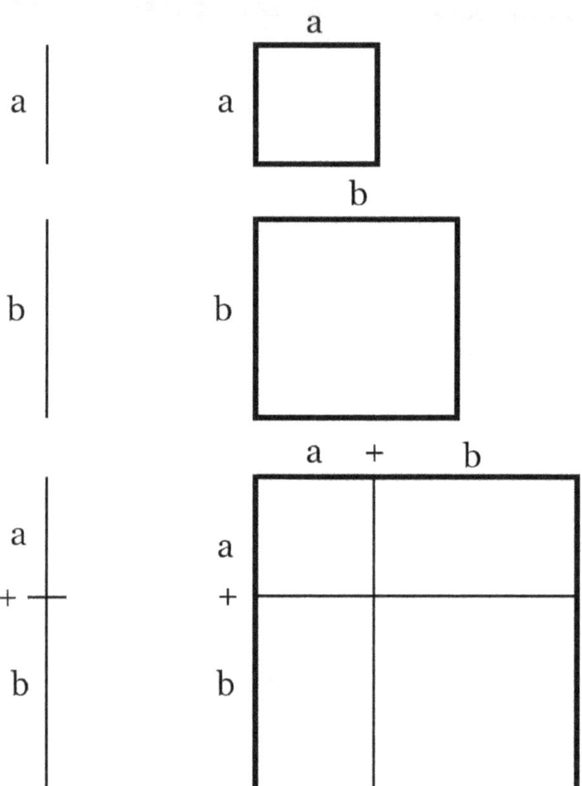

To make the sum of the squares we need to do something to the first two squares which is not a reading challenge but a mathematical intuition which leads us at once to the fact found in (1) above: "the square of the sum is bigger than the sum of the squares."

In both cases, the randomness of the choice of *a* and *b* creates a feeling that the last statement in the previous paragraph is always true although one sees only one example in front of oneself. Of course, this feeling does not result from either "R_3" or "R_4" but from a common sense experience brought with us to all intellectual activities from our early childhood when we noted that nouns — that is, words referring to concepts — are labels for *classes* of individuals and not for one individual. If nothing had been said above about *a* and *b* besides their initial definition (*a* number or *a* length) nothing would be assumed and thus the generality of the statements above would be experienced like it is in the statement: "these are houses" which is acceptable whatever the color, size or style, of each.

The indefinite article *a* (or *an)* is experienced as indefinite precisely because we all know that "a glass" or "a man" is said instead of "any glass" or "any man." In a mathematical statement like "the medians of *a* triangle are concurrent. . ." we clearly relate to the language in a special manner. We are aware that we have to relate first to an indefinite triangle (because of *a)* and then to the definite objects in it called medians (because of *the)* — objects three in number and thought of all at once. First we evoke in turn — separately and carefully — what each word requires of us and then what the words together mean — attributes of "R_3." But then we take the initiative of holding the given statement in our minds beyond this point in order to receive the meaning of the end of the statement. This can be described as "suspending judgment" until we know whether or not the given statement is true. Once we do know it is true, then we retain it as true in all cases and at all times. These are attributes of "R_4"in mathematics.

When we teach mathematics, we have to become adept at such analyses of statements and make our students aware of the special demands of "R_4" in this field. Once we have such awarenesses our retention of words will not be memorization but will result from having created in our minds new structures with their special dynamics. These are part of the acts which mathematize reality — that area of reality which holds together dynamically representatives of infinite classes of some concepts. "R_4" in mathematics is a biased reading because of its special property which calls in at the same time both *infinity and dynamics.*

To help students acquire "R_4" in mathematics, teachers must themselves practice reading statements not only for content but also for finding what the statement demands that students must do mentally in order to replace their "R_3" with the proper "R_4." Once they have done the mental work ("R_4") they can read mathematics as they do any spontaneous writing ("R_3"). All we can do here is merely suggest the means of reaching "R_4" in the two examples above.

"R_4" In Social Studies

The social studies ask a very different approach than does mathematics. A great deal more memorization is required of information presented through the unchangeable medium of print — names of persons, places, dates, or estimates of quantities. In mathematics many variables exist, while in the social studies students are presented with definite and untouchable data for retention.

Ogdens of course will have to be paid for such retention but, since more than separate items needs to be held in one's memory, students will have to acquire different techniques for the "R_4" in these areas of study.

History

When one is learning *history,* "R_3" will provide the skills for reading the stories it involves. But if total retention is required, the payment of ogdens will be necessary. The means that "R_4" will ask each reader to scan the statements slowly with a conscious acknowledgment that it is "engraving" each word in one's memory. At the end of each paragraph another conscious involvement is called for to ascertain that one is capable of "re-citing" what had been read — not necessarily with the same words of the text but with words that have an equivalent meaning.

Faithful retention is at first constructed carefully. The reader with the feeling of an "excavator" lifts the contents of the paragraph and moves them to a storage place in the mind. A sense of that proper functioning will accompany this type of reading and will become also a characteristic of an adequate "R_4" in this field.

Readers will not ask whether they are doing the work properly. What is experienced is that the scanning results in retention and that the retention is secured by merely stopping and feeling that the content referred to is actually there ready to trigger its re-gurgitation using equivalent speech. Recitation thus becomes re-citation.

In the study of history the extent of retention soon becomes considerable, since students are asked to work on as much as thirty pages from voluminous history texts in one sitting. Behind this school request is the belief that one is benefited by acquiring vast chunks of the accumulated collective experience of the culture — and doing so by rapidly committing it to memory.

Retaining "historical facts" includes a sense of certainty that what one holds in one's mind conforms to what the historian — based on his study of the field — has deposited in the narrative one has been reading. Conformity applies to the names, figures, attributes, comments and judgments, the makeup of situations, tactics and strategies, hierarchies of power and importance and so forth — each requiring a complex of blendings of mental components.

"R_4" in history asks for a vigilance which intelligence supports. It requires swift judgments about what is read and its consistencies. It demands a triggering of images — furnished, bright and glamorous — made dynamic by a disciplined imagination. These images include marching armies, fierce battles, coronations, gatherings for making treatises, court assemblies, parliamentary debates, assassinations, elections, budgets, alliances, and scores of other classifications of images that can help the students to store facts in their proper mental "boxes" where they are easily accessible.

"R_4" is the orchestration of the mental material supplied by the scanning of successive sentences, pictures, and diagrams which fill the pages of history books. After finishing reading short or long sections from these books, a reader must consult with oneself to ascertain if the content of one's mind reflects what had been scanned for retention. It then appears that the story held in one's mind makes sense in a number of ways because of criteria one has gathered by living one's own life in one's own circumstances and environment. These criteria help retention but also can show one that, except for a few adjustments, it is mainly "R_3" which is used in the reading of the stories of history.

"R_4" for history requires the retention of events in chronological order through the formation of a time-line. Reading history properly demands that this order exist by providing content which forces its formation. Hence the mind must come to that reading having prepared itself with a mental structure that handles durations as lengths which can overlap, which can follow each other to indicate precedence of one over others, or which can be unrelated or unconnected. Successions of actors on the historic scene — whether rulers or their aides, or peoples of various generations affecting each other for good or evil — must be kept in their place on the timeline. Although past actions can affect future happenings, these cannot change the past. They may still have an effect on the readers who suddenly realize the importance of particular actions and events — for example, because of the disclosure of some secret.

"R_4" in history may demand some experiential maturity. It requires developing some imagination to make sense of the hidden dynamics implied in the actions of some people who manage to reach power and to use it for their own ends — ends which may be catastrophic for all the others.

"R_4" in history may require that one limit the memories of history to a string of neutral facts. The new sense that comes from long reflection on the human condition — on passions and greed, on the springs of selfish action and of limited intelligence — cannot be easily made part of "R_4" in this field and may require another "*R*" beyond "R_4."

Actually, the content of history books is biased in a number of ways and most "facts" reported in them are colored by a priori viewpoints and prejudices of the writers. Still, as far as the functioning of "R_4" here is concerned, we can safely state that whether or not the truth of the text is fully supported by the critical examination of later historians, what the reader has extracted from reading the text can be considered as a way of using oneself that yields "R_4." Identifying oneself with what is left in oneself after reading and giving it the attribute of truth, also goes beyond "R_4." The problem is no longer how we can increase the yield of "R_4" in the case of history — which we have just outlined — but an "*R*" which is concerned with what is the proper definition of truth in history and truth in reporting it.

Geography

Social studies include *geography,* usually human geography, aiming at making students know their habitat with certain attributes: resources, climate, demography, trade, topography and so forth.

One new component appears which makes the difference between history and geography. In the latter what is stressed is the environment as it *now is,* rather than how it *has come to be* what it is. Instead of looking at the human environment solely as the result of earlier human actions — as is done in history — it may help us to establish that we see the geographic environment when we look at the objective content of our collective perceptions and express them in agreed upon terms referring to measurements and to the various categories of collections. One aspect of this work has been recorded best in the form of maps, and "R_3" in geography includes learning to read maps. These are drawn rather than written, but this drawing implies conventions and agreements as much as writing does. For instance, the images of maps we carry within our minds cannot be images of the reality since this requires us to be above the surface of the earth at a certain distance and with a certain visibility.

Scale affects our judgments directly. In order to sustain some thoughts about the environment relevant to geography, a particular scale is right. Changing it in either direction may distort perception and judgment. Hence "R_4" in geography requires the additional skill of reading maps and associating this with the narrative which accompanies these in textbooks.

The first request to students may be that they form a good picture of the map being studied — scanning the space it covers, focusing on colors, lines, labels, and sensing that all has been photographed in the mind. The second step is to move to the text and relate the narrative paragraph by paragraph to the visual information which is contained in the map — displayed in this form because it cannot be verbalized economically. In this way the students acquire the innards of the techniques needed for this "R_4" and gain an expertise with future paragraphs that improves the yield per scanning — that is, increases retention of material associated with a particular content at a sufficient level of understanding.

The kind of imagination called for as part of "R_4" in geography, is different from that mentioned in the case of history, and it must be cultivated and improved by studying more geography. It refers to the replacement of words by images which begin by being maps or parts of them and then become evocations of the realities referred to through both words and maps. For example, the statement: "The rain forests along the wide river Amazon are sparsely populated but are shelter to teeming animal species," works on these three levels. It clearly belongs to the field of geography because the word "Amazon" imposes on the reader the map of Brazil and Venezuela. If it is remembered per se, the information in it belongs solely to that subject matter. But these few words could also trigger images closely connected with stories and pictures. However, if the stories and pictures have only been part of studying geography at school, they may only be remembered vaguely as knowledge acquired "indirectly" and therefore incapable of being re-created by one's mind to enhance the meaning of this statement.

Geography also asks us to remember associations which are only necessary outside of the human components. For example, the existence of diamond and gold mines is a part of the geologic description of how the earth was formed over a billion years of cooling. But the fact that some of them exist in Kimberley, South Africa and others in Soviet Russia inserts a human component and transforms the geological statements into geographical ones. "Copper" may trigger in geography, Chile, Zaire and Zambia, while it may trigger in physics conductors, wires, and electrical lines. "R_4" is one process which creates such associations for the purpose of retention. Most of our present knowledge is necessarily such that it can be generated in this way.

Because of the trends in human political affairs, a great deal of geographic knowledge will have to be such that it can be discarded and restructured. "R_4" will therefore have this additional attribute. It enables the mind to cancel old associations and hold on to new ones. For example, there are no longer Dutch colonies in Southeast Asia, and German colonies, existing during Word War I, were taken over by the League of Nations and some of them have become sovereign countries with new names and new flags. Only elderly people can recall the former names of these colonies and in so doing inject history into geography.

Economics

Social studies include other specialized disciplines. For example, *economics* — the so-called "dismal science" — remains for most people marginal knowledge although it is intimately connected with the lives of all of us. Because of this, "R_4" in economics takes on an appearance which distinguishes it from the "R_4" encountered in history and geography.

First of all, "R_3" is unable to serve us as it did in history. Economics is a new science seeking crisper definitions through finding its own few cardinal concepts which can be arranged in an appropriate hierarchy. And since this is not yet the case, ambiguities prevail. Confusions are common and retention is not helped by uncertainty. There are so many components affecting the quantities which are to be expressed in mathematical terms that no constants can be used to provide the bases of calculations. A science normally is expected to make reliable predictions. In economics this is less and less possible mainly because a number of unexpected items need constantly to be taken into account.

If the only thing required in the study of economics is a study of facts relating to the past behavior of the economy in sovereign countries, it is possible to write coherently and for readers to make use of the "R_4" of history in reading this "economic history." But if the intent is to use "R_4" to become an economist (whatever this word may mean) one has to find what kind of reading will be required so that one ends up functioning as an economist — that is, like those who write the texts one has to study.

Economists as professionals are of course free to use, as they do, any one of the instruments accessible to them in order to make sense of those present trends affecting in the near future the economies under consideration — mathematics, statistics, computer programs, surveys, classifications, graphings, extrapolations, analyses, syntheses, hunches. Hence, a special preparation not easily obtained may be required for reading economic literature. Often a preparation valid for some texts is not valid as preparation for some others. This is so not only because of the techniques required, but because in this field beliefs and even mental make-ups act as obstacles to comprehension. It is no longer only a matter of paying ogdens but of agreeing to surrender to a different set of presuppositions which act as foundations for the scientific quest in question. "R_4" will be developed while working: an "R_4" not transferable to other fields, even to other social sciences. In so far as it must involve items which are also part of history and geography, "R_4" in economics may already have been partially cultivated. In so far as quantified entities can be treated mathematically, "R_4" in economics would already be at hand because of what is known of "R_4" in mathematics. But in so far as the axioms and definitions of economics lack the obviousness of the mathematical ones, their acceptance may be resisted and the deductions doubted. "R_4" in economics would not necessarily trigger consent and therefore may require an artificial retention difficult to maintain. This short-term memory may lead to no acquisition of knowledge at all because the reader believes he has *not* read what his own mind can not organically re-generate. In contrast, if one comes to writings which are akin to one's own thinking then that kind of retention will show itself which is in fact the facility of regenerating contact by deductions, and "R_4" will be much more an "R_3" than a new way of reading.

In this last remark we find how acquisition of knowledge is possible in economics through encountering concepts which, because they agree with one's own prejudices, quickly become the foundation of one's thinking and then deduction produces the system one adheres to. Often one's politics stems from these sources and when this happens economics and politics affect each other. When the concepts oppose one's prejudices, no acquisition of knowledge follows except through rote learning. Then, because it has been memorized, it can be tested in schools but it cannot serve functionally for attacking problems.

One profitable way of using "R_4" in this field may be obtained by simulating acceptance of a certain set of premises and then generating its corresponding economic systems by deduction. Such exercises may make us into readers of economics literature understanding *why* systems differ, and perhaps also where we stand personally on these matters.

But because economics is a very complex field in which dormant variables become dominant and conversely, "R_4" will reveal new ways of working of man's mind. Into these the reader injects his own variables and creates new systems. This raises the question whether a reading that is creative still can be considered to be "R_4"?

"R_4" In the Natural Sciences

Much more room will be required than we have here to describe adequately "R_4" in physics, chemistry and biology. All we can hope to achieve here is to characterize basically *the modes of thought* which sustains these sciences and qualify the reading that yields functional knowledge in those three fields.

Physics

Physics is the study of the phenomena of nature in which energy is the essential concept and variable. When the *scale* of the phenomena is that of the energy directly accessible to man and handled by him personally, understanding what one reads in that science appeals to an imagination most people can develop or use. Hence "R_4" is "R_3" plus the formation of schemas abstracted from one's own actions — of which everyone can be aware. Physics then becomes essentially *mechanics*.

Since all the concepts of mechanics can be reached by awareness of our body involved in the many actions we find ourselves performing every day, it is possible to teach "R_4" — that is, to acquire a knowledge of mechanics — by illustrating the statements found in mechanics books with our own actions. What we do with our various levers (arms, legs, jaws); what we do when we improve our throws; what we do to open a jar, and so forth, all help us make sense of what we read. And not only that, for we can see how our imagination combines these concepts to create simple machines, canals and sluices, and communicating pipes. We can notice how we transform our physical energy into those forms we need and cannot obtain through our skeleton and muscles: pulleys, cogged wheels, brakes and accelerators, balancing systems, cranes and so on. Our mass and our inertia, the composition of forces, elasticity, momentum, kinetic and potential energies, can all be defined by simple experiments which make us aware of the many things we can do with our own bodies and our muscular energy.

This section of physics (historically developed before all others) uses awareness of physical energy in our systems but there are others which follow from awarenesses called observations: observations of shadows, of light, of sounds (and of the sensorial properties of sounds, such as pitch and intensity) of roughness and smoothness of tenseness and slackness and so forth. All of these will serve to begin the other chapters of physics we find in textbooks under the labels of optics, acoustics, elasticity, resistance. "R_4" in these chapters means precisely this: coming into contact with the awarenesses which generate the bases for the phenomena written about. It is these awarenesses which provide the true meanings behind the words printed and the diagrams drawn. Unless we can make sense within of how forces and levels of energy work, we cannot project them outside ourselves, into the contrived experiments forming the bulk of physical knowledge. Only through this process of projection of what the reader's mind found in the text, can understanding of physics take place. This is the mechanism of "R_4" in that field. Without it, readers, by using "R_3," will only lift words out of the printed pages and state that the matter is "above their heads." But with it, "R_4" becomes the "R_3" of physicists.

* * *

The other *two scales* come into physics when we extend our study of nature to the cosmic and microscopic universes respectively. In both cases physics works on *models* produced by the theoretical physicists, and what is written about them requires a new "R_4" to be acquired by people other than the authors of the theories.

The usual passage from the scale of mechanics to the other two scales is done through mathematics rather than through the somatic experiences mentioned above. What was possible in the human scale when it was made into mathematical equations (of different kinds: differential, partial differential, tensorial, operator, matrix and algebras etc.) allowed the perception that the scale could as easily be reduced or magnified, and this leads to a grasp of reality in which perception was purely through the intellect and no longer through the senses. Metaphors are used to bridge the gap for those who cannot relate directly to what is behind the mathematics. Thus readers use images valid at the human scale to reach what is not perceptible. "R_4" requires this extra facility of not taking words literally and of becoming capable of accepting new disciplines of thinking required by the ways thinkers propose their models.

Thus, we can understand the meaning of specializing as a nuclear physicist, a cosmologist, or an astrophysicist — and consider that everybody who wishes it may acquire such specialties.

"R_4" in physics can be facilitated by insisting that *physics,* even at our scale, *is a study of models.* And as a result students are helped in their studies of nature. When readers have (as second nature) the ability to replace statements by the dynamic relationship of entities which are linked by the rules defining the models, what they imagine as real *is* the reality of physical models. To grasp this reality they will use instruments and probes created specifically in order to make perceptible on our scale the effects of some additions or subtractions of energy however small or large each one is.

Chemistry

"R_4" in *chemistry* demands another kind of adjustment. In that science, what is studied is the transformation of matter as expressed in its composition and reflected in the various formulae. Although there is an aspect of chemistry which can be acquired mainly by "R_3" plus some bias which replaces contents found in nature with pure substances (called atoms and molecules) — an aspect which today can more properly be seen as a historical introduction to chemistry — modern chemistry is both a new language and a new mode of thought requiring its own "R_4."

This language is one of formulae and reactions. For example, H_2O is to be read "h two owe" or "water," though nothing in the formula says it is the water we know and drink. Thus the "R_3" of chemistry will include new reflexes, *decoding* the "chemical words" with their now conventional notation and evoking that substance as it has been obtained from laboratories and not from the nature we know in our everyday life. There are hundreds of thousands of chemical "words" each *able* to tell its name in a less arbitrary way than do ordinary English words (as we saw above with H_2o). When such a name is uttered or written, it is recognizable by any informed chemist and the usage is considered "good."

In fact, this was the case so long as the complexity of these "words" was manageable. Soon (when organic chemistry was established and advanced) that became too cumbersome and first a "shorthand" and then a "slang" were introduced. "Aspirin" is a popular name for acetylsalicylic acid whose spelling is O-CH_3-CO-C_6H_4-COOH. Chemists prefer chemical spellings because they provide a great deal of information about the "word." But like everyone else they cannot easily retain long strings of merged sounds and they invent shortcuts. The nomenclature of chemistry has been generated to blend the maximum of information with the greatest economy of language, particularly in organic chemistry where molecules may have hundreds of thousands of atoms. DNA is the best known example. But there are many others.

A great deal of attention is placed in learning to read "chemical words," upon those segments of the words which serve to provide testimony of "chemical functions" of the substances concerned. *Radicals* in the formulae of some molecules tell something about the substance they are purported to represent in a way analogous to what prefixes and suffixes do for ordinary words. Thus acids, bases, alcohols, amins and so forth are as recognizable to chemists as "words" written as adverbs and gerunds are to grammarians, except that there are many more of those in chemistry. "R_4" consists in part in developing a sensitivity to the morphology of the "words" and to the multiple classifications which embrace them.

But we can take the language of chemistry one step further, concerning ourselves with syntax and semantics. Some associations of "words" are permissible and among these some are meaningful. The associations or *chemical reactions* are selective: only "words" expressing these can be put together to produce the phrases which hold together organically. By reading the "reactions" students develop a sense of how to expand the language further and further. To become a chemist is not only to have memorized the numerous reactions that fill the chemistry books but to have noticed the behavior of reactions and surmise their outcome; to have acquired a sense of what can be done with the given to get the new even if, as in ordinary speech, one uses again and again the same "words."

"R_4" in chemistry will allow the acquisition of existing knowledge as an expanse of analyzed substances expressible in chemical language. But more than this, it will offer the acquisition of a universe made of transformations controlled by analysis and synthesis. In the latter is enshrined the semantics of chemistry: only those who know how to make sense of structure can manage to produce *new* meanings in the form of new substances.

If the teaching of chemistry can be perceived as teaching the "R_4" of that science — that is reading words, phrases, sentences, stresses, intonations, and then compounding units to generate vaster ones (as far as that can go) — more students would see the fascination present in the chemical literature which has allowed us to have a man-made environment. This, thanks to chemistry can be more and more functional and serve man's ends. The arcane appearance of chemistry will then be replaced by the poetry of a reality perceived everywhere in the material universe — our habitat. "R_4" can contribute this here as well as in the other fields.

Biology

Biology being the study of life, a new dimension for "R_4" appears with this science. Although biology is based on chemical and physical phenomena which can be described in a written text, as we learned in the previous two sections, *the mode of thought* of biologists is sui generis. "R_4" will require that this be taken into account.

Life is still a mystery and remains irreducible to premises which are only physicochemical. One of the main differences is that all phenomena in biology are "temporal." Time is of the essence. Not only by the channel of evolution but because there is a beginning and an end to all that the mind entertains in biology: death is copresent with existence and viability means perduration.

To learn to read biology is to acquire that dimension of thinking which maintains the question of viability at the center. Something can be started by physical or chemical means, but would it go on? Every step taken to ascertain this will belong to biology. Hence, biology will, on the one hand, integrate physics and chemistry (though not in order to produce purely physical or chemical phenomena) and on the other, subordinate them to the ultimate end of understanding life with its various and numerous manifestations.

Though it seems that biology is more complex than either physics or chemistry, those who choose to specialize in it only need to borrow from those sciences what makes things clearer to them. They are predisposed to keep life as the climate of all their thinking and find their satisfaction in the presence of this dimension. Hence they will spontaneously accept the discipline of reading which goes to form "R_4" in biology.

For those who do not envisage becoming biologists, but read biology texts for exam purposes, "R_3" and memorization may be sufficient. They will acquire biological knowledge as they do all other knowledge of school subjects. They can easily forget it or hold it in their memory for reference, but not necessarily to use it to unravel any one of the many marvels and mysteries present in the studies of life on earth.

"R_4" in every field will be the proper way of reading if what it yields is an increase of experience recognizable as similar to their own by those who dedicate themselves to that field. The special jargon only serves as one of the criteria for this recognition. The inner climate and the insights displayed in the spontaneous statements are the true ingredients which tell that one can read *and* understand the singularity of the mode of thought that sustains that field and generates its scientific examinations.

In the case of biology, to provide this climate and a number of these insights — that is, for an education which will produce the proper "R_4" in the case of reading what biologists write — we must suggest exercises also sui generis.

This is equivalent to learning to put certain kinds of questions and to attempting to find adequate answers.

One of them could be: "Why do flamingos stand on only one leg? Are there other animals with such behavior? Is it in order to rest? Could man try out such a stand and through this decide whether the choice of such a behavior is determined by the fact that one can rest well on one leg?"

One could repeat without any understanding and any sense that it is a meaningful matter: "flamingos and marabous rest on only one of their two legs." This is attainable by "R_3" alone. But to make it belong to "R_4" a reader must feel that it is a striking behavior, worthy of note, worthy of being entertained for a while longer and becoming in one's mind: "How do we know? Is this true? How do we come to such a conclusion? and with what certainty?"

It is no longer only a matter of paying ogdens (which is necessary to associate the words "flamingos" and "marabous" with this retained statement) but one of finding a whole alchemy of the mind. There is little mechanical in life, though perhaps it seems a lot. It has taken three centuries to organize the classifications of botany and zoology so that they could be memorized in order to form a frame of reference for the study that followed. Such learning is not actually concerned with insights into life, only in recognizing similarities and differences and in noting both.

The similarities serve to form the broad categories in which things perceptibly different are seen as *not* different such as marsupials, whales and rhinoceros all being seen as mammals. In this the categories are being looked at *abstractly* in the logical terms of "inclusion of classes." The end of these sciences is complex classifications leading to a stress on differences as the way to separate the billions of individuals from each other.

There is room of course, for an "R_4" which will provide students with -

1 a retention of the work done over these centuries, and

2 with frames of reference indispensable for further study.

But it is not very different from what we met in history, economics and chemistry. The specific "R_4" for biology begins when the readers know that everything they read refer to life and makes them maintain contact with all the phenomena of life. For instance, it is "R_4" when readers realize that every thought they may have may require recasting on the basis of a new light brought into the field either by a new observation or a new insight. That is to say when they become aware that the knowledge one reaches is susceptible to sudden variation and therefore must be suspended. "R_4" in biology must be more critical in the above sense and based on the awarenesses -

1 that there is no absolute truth in any statements in this field, and

2 that one has to find out how much of the biological truth is accessible to the scientist and students reading the reports of the scientists.

"Comprehensive reading" is more descriptive of "R_4" in biology.

Special exercises must be devised in order to prepare students for such comprehensive reading which merges *information* (from chemistry, taxonometry, anatomy, physiology, microscopy, ecology etc.) *evocation of dynamic images* (so that it is known that what is being considered is in space but variable with time) *theoretical biases* (such as "natural selection," adaptation, recapitulation, etc.) Their main function must be to keep the students' minds alerted to the meaning of "fact" in biology. Behind what can be photographed, which obviously is factual, what can be examined under magnifying instruments (from lenses to electron microscopes) and obviously leads to perceptible physical facts, there *are* facts special to biology which answer the questions of how? why? and for what purpose?

For example:

1 the extinction of species, which deals with what is no longer there and raises both its own challenges and a challenge to the non-extinct species;

2 the generation of new species;

3 the incredible variety of the flora and fauna on earth — including how to understand their existence in terms of habitat, climate, and phenomena at the scale of the earth and of the local physicochemical conditions.

Only by stressing these large issues with students of biology will they develop a mode of thought that transcends the molecular scale as well as the scale of the earth — while integrating the findings at these scales and all the scales in between — and come to feel that their knowledge will become meaningful and worthy of being retained.

"R_4" is formed from "R_3" plus those processes of transcendence and integration. It is these processes that put into perspective the words scanned and the semantics associated with each statement.

It is perhaps in biology that "R_4" gains its greatest complexity and therefore shows which demands it makes on students supposed to acquire new knowledge through the use of "R_3." Teachers of biology have the opportunity to show their students which is the metamorphosis of "R_3" (already mastered) which will serve them best in their education as biologists. This ability to read and comprehend biology can live side by side with all the "R_4"s which we have seen can be generated as separate disciplines of reading.

* * *

This chapter has offered an outline of many fields of investigation and research still open to students of reading. In summing up we can say that a multitude of "R_4"s are generated due to the fact that

1 each field of human endeavor develops its own ways of reaching the contents of one's awarenesses;

2 this content, in so far as it differs from contents of other fields, will demand its own way of expressing itself and therefore of being communicated.

Part IV

Writing

9 Writing as an Instrument

The following group of chapters will consider what common sense teaches us about writing, the teaching of writing, and how it can be implemented so that all students benefit by it.

Already in the earlier sections we studied some components of writing. Chapter 6 was devoted to the teaching of spelling which of course only manifests itself when we attempt to put our spoken speech on paper. But we also mentioned in Chapters 3 to 5, that we look at writing as the intermediary between speaking and reading. This means that in putting down the fleeting speech to make it more permanent, using several conventions, writing comes a split second before we test with our eyes that this transmutation has actually taken place — a test which is part of reading.

The act of writing requires that our hand obeys specific orders to shape the letters forming the words and hence the sentences which include them.

To educate our hand to do this job presents us with a scholarly aspect called "penmanship." Many of us have spent years trying to master that art with lamentable final results. A few of us end up owning a beautiful handwriting admired by all.

Copying designs made of the letters on the word charts or from the primers (beginning with R_o) is cultivated by Visual Dictation #1 and made autonomous by Visual Dictation #2, before it becomes part of Visual Dictation #3 and is called "creative writing."

Therefore we have already worked on writing at a few levels. Students using our materials may not find capital letters used on our charts and booklets, they may not be fully aware of the meaning and role of punctuation until they have completed "R_3," but they are likely to have acquired a great deal of know-how about the task of putting thousands of statements on paper.

If these statements are creations of theirs — though restricted to what can be done with the words contained in the word charts as they are met one by one — we can claim that at least one aspect of writing has already been given attention. Our students know how to arrange the words they design: on horizontal lines, the signs from left to right and the lines from top to bottom, leaving space between consecutive words and occasionally adding the sign "?" every time they hear their reading produce a question.

They can be made to think that what they put down can be read by others simply by asking classmates to exchange the papers on which they have written the exercises based on the word charts.

This will provide the opportunity to gain good penmanship on the basis of "charity." Indeed, if we think of others we have a good reason to improve our ways of putting down the letters of the words and the words of the sentences, so that they are *legible*. To succeed in this charitable movement we need to find approaches to holding the writing instruments and shaping the individual letters that attempt to fuse our qualities of temperament and speed of speech with these mechanical components — being concerned only about producing the least objectionable results until we become vulnerable to other components such as the aesthetic.

The writing exercises at these stages are producing other awarenesses as well.

Slowly but surely we discover that sentences are units, that conjunctions articulate clauses, that some thoughts require more words than others to be expressed in writing; and that the length of sentences is dictated by the thoughts which originate them. Later on we shall scrutinize these connections and find the merits and demerits of short and long sentences according to the contents *and* the kind of audience we are addressing. But already, at this stage we can become aware of our statements being related to our inner states, perceivable only by us but made doubly objective when expressed in spoken words and then in writing.

We can become aware that words "pull" each other when we are forming statements and that such associations between words exist already in the spoken language. In this, we also find that the order of the words corresponds to the order in which they come to mind, and that it is this sequence which makes the statements *sound right*. Later on, this awareness will also lead us to reach the meaning of the *correctness* of statements, and still later, to find the *grammatical rules* which can be extracted from the spoken language and projected onto the written one.

Every time we scan the word charts we can make choices. In this we become aware that having selected one or two words, that something in them conditions the order of the following choices, and that this selection leads to what is called *the structure* of the statement and contributes as much as the words to conveying meaning.

The conditioning also leads to the awareness that words have *functions*, and that there are only a small number of these functions. We then feel that we know these functions innerly: that is, we have inner criteria which will make us sense that if such and such a word is called an "adjective" or a "noun" or a "verb," many others will have those same properties. Then we do not err in the way we qualify them. Other words are "adverbs" because they qualify verbs, and innerly we know how. Some words replace nouns and are called "pronouns" of which there are several categories: the possessive, the demonstrative, the personal, the interrogative, the relative — each determined by a definite criterion, other than the capacity to replace nouns which generate other meanings. There are also other words whose function is to link, or to express definiteness and indefiniteness, or to place events relatively in time and space: "articles" and "prepositions."

All this output from the word charts and Visual Dictation #2 represents a bonus when we aim mainly to do what we did between "R_0" and "R_3" i.e. to teach reading fluently, with comprehension but also with specific by-products as we met them in Chapters 7 and 8. The bonus is a new relation of ours to the language: an acquaintance with what it does: how and, perhaps even, why it does it. This relation may have a future in establishing in us criteria which will help us become more articulate as speakers and writers by finding entries into the language which go beyond the ordinary expression and communication of everyday life, and sensing potentials in the language which the literature has exploited in becoming what it is. We can own some of these potentials, and work at developing them to the point of becoming writers — and do so not only for ourselves.

To this point, we have looked at the written language in so far as it can become the instrument of our own expression and provide us with the means of making that expression consciously our own and of using it for what the more permanent written form makes possible. Our own thoughts and feelings, our aspirations and realizations, our examinations of issues and events, our projections, dreams, and intuitions can now be given objective form and be sent away to be looked at by anyone on our planet. The written language, being the product of our own productivity, will give us chances to add to the existing literature and enable us to make our own contribution to the collective awareness of man and his destiny.

Awareness that we can use teaching to bring everyone to the boundary between

1 what is part of the necessary components of the mastery of the written language, and

2 what is inalienably individual and unique

must be integrated into the *Common Sense of Teaching Writing*.

The *art of writing* can only be exemplified, not taught. As has always been the case, every writer will make a personal journey. But teachers can maximize the chances of students stepping over that boundary which separates the area of the "how" from the area of the "what."

Common sense tells us not to stifle inspiration by only thinking of form and format, of respect for tradition, and of the imitation of selected models. But common sense also tells us that we should try to make every speaker who has something worthwhile to say, say it, while providing him with those means which serve both expression and communication.

To this task we devote the balance of this book.

* * *

First, we shall look into the conditions for becoming a writer. Then, we shall provide as many exercises as are necessary to awaken the awareness that one can be a writer, and, more than this, are sufficient to attempt the first trials. Finally, we shall entertain some common sense views which have been found helpful by a number of people who worked with us over the years — some of whom have been very successful with their own students at colleges or in elementary and high schools.

We shall only use our own work to illustrate our suggestions, leaving readers to find in the literature of the field of writing other sources of inspiration and of practice.

10 We All Have Something to Say

It does not take much to catch ourselves having every day, on a number of occasions, the opportunity of changing into words our thoughts and experiences. If we watch ourselves in our familiar surroundings with our relatives and friends, we shall not fail to find that we are articulate on a large number of familiar topics such as our likes and dislikes, our assessment of people who come and go in our lives, our judgment of ordinary or extraordinary events which are close to us or of local, regional, national or even global magnitude. If we examine our vocabulary we will find that we possess words which are capable of describing most situations in which we find ourselves.

This first awareness of ourselves as people having something to say and saying it on so many occasions, is the most primitive one. It is also the most important one when we want to generate in a group of students the basis for involvement in a writing course.

We all take for granted that there is a place for speech, and that using it every day for so many varied functions, is natural and therefore of no special significance for us even in other circumstances. Still, who could deny that before we would put anything down on paper we must have had it available in the spoken medium? The fleeting property of the spoken language and the properties of language which make many expressions equivalent, distract us from the relationship between the stable permanent written paragraphs and the evanescence of speech. In terms of temporal hierarchies, the spoken language was invented before its written form. They are deeply related, at least to the inventors of the various transcriptions. We could perhaps learn something from that initial link, in our studies of writing and its teaching.

That is why we begin the second part of this book with the first awareness we want to force within our students.

If we can make our students aware of the source of the flow of words in them we shall be able to concern ourselves with the main obstacles in them, which is that alone in front of a blank sheet of paper they so often find nothing in them to put down. The artifact of giving a topic for a composition may work for some and at a certain stage. It seems much more reasonable and certainly handier, to lead everyone to recognize that in our spoken speech words pour out spontaneously, well-organized, and generally acceptable to us as the equivalent of what we think, want or feel. If we could easily capture that flow and transmute it into the written form, we would reach the awareness that not only do we have something to say all day but also something to write.

Such simplification of the challenge will be put right later when we look at the objectified speech and find in it a great deal to work on in specific manners, for determined purposes. But we do not want to lose the great value of the awareness just encountered by our students and for our students.

The awareness that any writing has its source in a sequence of statements verbalizing what one experiences is affectively liberating. Once this stage is reached, it makes available energy needed to take oneself further on the road to entering writing with some confidence and understanding, and the task for teachers and students is much easier.

For example, if a teacher can manage to tape what students say on occasions when they are excited about some matter and permit a flow of words to come to them and be spoken, and if these words are then transcribed by the teacher and read to the class on a subsequent occasion, it is likely that some students will be surprised and jolted from their retrenched position and reduce their resistance to writing. The result will be that some students who had questioned their ability will join the group of those who have already moved toward becoming writers.

An advantage of this approach to the matter concerned is that the intervention of the teacher allows the definite affective problem to be reached and to be worked on specifically. The weaknesses of the text in terms of spelling, say, will not show up and thereby threaten the positive condition into which students have been put in order to permit their movement towards emotional freedom.

What we want to work on is the awareness that *almost all students have something to say*. But once this is understood by them, we will still have to embark on the way to induce them to become writers, we need not defeat our ends by accumulating obstacles in front of those who fear writing. Anyone who considers that a first or early writing has to be free of blemishes should be kept from teaching such classes. Like a loving supporter, we can learn to look at the positive contribution of the work done to the awareness that in writing there is a component that resembles speech and that the first condition for a writing to exist is that it has been willed and unfolded in time. Whether it is the writer himself or a secretary who puts it down, is not important in the beginning.

Of course, the students who have no problems in writing are already aware that they have something to put down even if what they produce may lack qualities that make it attractive to others. These students are not part of the group challenging us here. Later we shall consider their work for components other than making it happen — our theme here.

If we look at the students in writing classes as persons having many matters they are concerned with, it seems reasonable to consider first the motivation aspect and to enlist it in the students' education.

No doubt, there are many ways of motivating students to get into various tasks. If writing requires a steady mobilization for a while, the motivations needed to keep one going will take different forms in various cases.

There are students who know they have something to say but after writing their first paragraphs discover that they are emptied and abandon the task. They mistake the initial impulse for a thrust which will be sufficient to take them through. Such students need to know what they have to say and perhaps develop a sense of how long they can stand the pressure from the flow of what wants to be expressed without losing some of these thoughts. This will cause them to develop the discipline of jotting down the various points that come to them and to estimate vaguely (or accurately) how long it would take to develop each point on paper. Once this discipline exists there will be some correlation between the energy mobilized and its flow for the duration of the writing.

There are students who wish a priori to produce a composition satisfying criteria imposed by traditional teachers. They are mainly concerned with a structure — with a beginning, a middle and an end — not knowing exactly why there should be a structure or whether each of these three parts has a function reachable by common sense. For such students a study of texts that display the freedom of writers, as well as the many forms developed in all literatures, would serve to bring to their notice that rather than authoritative commands, it is originality, spontaneity which are the qualities that make writers select how they write. When such students feel paralyzed because they have not mastered the art of structuring, they go to join those incapacitated for other reasons. For them too, we need to bring to the fore that having something to say is more important than to obey a priori rules.

There are students whose minds are full of a prioris of other kinds: those who think that only if they are as good as the greatest writers would they set pen to paper; those who wish once they sit in front of a pad that their inspiration be endless and soon produce a large writing in the genre of their predilection; those who think that all writers are great writers and that they in no way can join them; and those who do not suspect that their ideas and views of the world are biased and may be discussed, and who refuse to expose themselves.

These students, and many of other categories, kinds or types, fill our writing classes and challenge us differently. All of them have to be served and the first condition for their producing some writing is that they gain a less complicated sight of the situation — or rather, a correct sight. For this to happen with more likelihood perhaps an exposition by the teacher that

1 thousands of books are published in their language every month or year,

2 only ten or so have a chance of being mentioned twenty or so years later, and those are not necessarily among the present best-sellers (a criterion to be examined closely),

3 unless one studies how writers write, one has no idea of how easily or painfully they produce their works,

4 writers write about what interest them and in a genre that suits them best,

5 writers and publishers guess what can interest others and gamble every time they issue a new book by a well-known writer or a newcomer to the scene,

6 many more writers submit works to publishers than are actually published, and thus writing and being in-print can be, and are, very different things.

Because of these remarks, perhaps, it should be known that, for most, writing is an end in itself: *to give a more permanent form to one's expression of what one can verbalize.* It is just for oneself. In some cases it may also be for others, but not necessarily.

And this will be an evolved meaning of "I have something to say."

11 Working On What We Put Down

One day perhaps we shall become so good at writing that we can personally take care of *all* the tasks involved in making our work as good as it can be.

But for now, having reached the conviction that our statements resemble what we have in mind — as much as we can make them do so unaided — we have taken care of the most important stage in the process of writing. This is true simply because we can touch and weigh the sheets of paper on which we deposited our thoughts and feelings, and we can attempt to open the door which makes them available to others.

As soon as this is accomplished there will be a new, most important involvement for the writer which is: in this work are there items that should not be there which manage to distract readers because they were not attended to during the act of writing? For example, are there

1 spelling mistakes the writer is unable to spot?

2 terms in the sentences which lead to ambiguities or to unwelcome interferences in the mind of the readers?

3 constructions of sentences that do not conform to what critics and teachers of English consider correct usage?

4 other awkward attributes of the form which need examination, and

5 words which give the statements qualities conflicting with the intentions of the writer and which could be replaced by others performing that purpose better?

All these and other questions open up for us news tasks in relation to writing that need to be worked on so as to give any final product a form that allows it to stand by itself and even be considered an improvement, and so as to increase the chances of each work performing its intended function with the readership.

In our Chapter on Spelling, we indicated that in the teaching of reading — and of the writing that goes with it — there are techniques and materials which may lead all students to the mastery of spelling. Either the writers we are considering here have already reached that stage — and only very exceptionally make a slip that can be labeled a spelling error — or they have a shaky background in spelling that needs attention.

Two attitudes on the part of the teacher are possible:

1 stop all work on writing and give an intensive course on spelling that will make the writers sensitive to spelling and better spellers because they are attentive to what matters in this area; that is being better watchers of the shape of words per se and of the rules that affect the form of words in certain circumstances, or

2 add to each writing session a session on the spelling concerned with the words which are not well spelled in the text in question, and find out what to do with the student who is not aware that these words should be written differently.

So long as there is a chance that the spelling weaknesses of a particular student can be coped with in this sporadic and ad hoc manner, then this approach can be continued. But if either frustration sets in because weaknesses cannot be reduced in this way or too much time is spent with only a certain number of words considered, it may be advisable to take the drastic step of involving students of writing in a thorough examination of the demands of spelling and in the exercises which lead to mastery for most. What this means is outlined in the chapters through Chapter 6.

Besides spelling, we may need to work on grammar with our students.

Our purpose will never be to steal time from writing to make our students into grammarians. This would produce a specialist, and we mean something quite different when we say we need work on grammar.

The grammar we are concerned with is found solely in that smooth unfolding of sentence after sentence so that any native speaker who is reading reaches the thoughts and feelings which have guided the writing without any interference from the structure adopted by the writer.

We already alluded to a way of creating awareness of how the English language behaves by making students realize that they already know that some things are never said in that language by anyone who knows how to speak. The choices of deliberate mistakes to force awareness are the teacher's.

For example: "That girl is short, but he is not short enough for that job," where the association of *he* with the feminine precludes its use here. Students will protest and suggest *she* for the pronoun.

Working on the same sentence we can produce some other deliberate errors; the second one is qualitatively different:

1. "That girl are short, but she are not short enough for that job," will also shock students to protest and ask for *is* to be substituted for *are,* while

2. "That girl is short, but she is not very short like she needs to be for that job," where it may not be noticed that *as* is preferred to *like* when the clause being introduced is a full one containing a verb.

The ambiguity related to the word *you,* because it can be singular or plural, has led many people to say "you was" instead of "you were" when addressing one person. Within the various dialects that distinguish the two uses of *you* by changing the verb, there is no objection to this usage. But across dialects, if we want to force awareness that a change is needed, we can only do it by working on the fact that two pronouns exist for the first and third person (singular and plural) but yet for the second person only one form exists — that is, the plural has been adopted for addressing *one or more* persons.

By those students who say "you was," finding for example, that they do not ever say "you loves" or "you has," they have an opportunity to stop and think about the basis for such a form in their own dialect.

Some people who learn the use of *did* in the formation of the past, still do not feel that such an ambiguous word, which serves as a substitute for so many verbs (as in "yes, I did" meaning *give, take, go. . .*) can carry by itself the reference to the past, they may say, "I did went" instead of "I did go," simply because "went" refers in their mind to the past while "did" does not.

The subtleties connected with the verb *to do* pose problems to speakers and writers alike. The addition of "do" and "does" in "I do go" or "she does come," alters the emphasis, but occupies one's mind differently than the addition of "did" to "I go."

In some dialects "he does," becomes "he do," possibly because of the polite requests "do come. . ." and "do go. . ." often heard.

By making people reflect on the existence of such subtleties and by putting into circulation what is accepted across dialects as well as what we want to warn them about, we may enhance the attention given to these usages and encourage students to adopt the forms recommended by best writers in English in their formal writing.

Clearly, people are in the field of grammar at as many levels of awareness as we found they are in the field of spelling, although most of the correct spoken expressions do not get challenged when written down while spelling is immediately an issue when the words are written down. Grammar refers to the spirit of the language developed historically which will be lost if modified. Spelling on the other hand could be changed by a government decree so that if we wished, all words could be written as pronounced (that is, phonetically) — and without affecting the spirit of the language.

Such a study only requires self awareness on the part of students or teacher.

I may see that there are connections between my feelings and the words I use; between my thoughts, my premonitions, my worries, my intentions, my projects, my reflections on events, my doubts; and between my needs to feel companionship, to feel I am not alone or the only one experiencing this or that, or to be concerned with this or that. I can relate to those connections in order to know which ones are sources for the statements I utter to others, or even to myself. I can relate to them in order to reach the verbal forms which are spontaneously triggered in me by my particular mood, by the person or persons I talk to or imagine I am talking with. I can notice in what ways changing subject or changing interlocutors affect my flow of words or my particular choice of vocabulary.

Can I see that there are many ways of expressing myself according to whether:

1 I am talking to peers, to younger people, to older people or socially "superior" people;

2 I am evoking some scene, imagining a story, or telling a joke;

3 I am controlling what I say and how I say it because of the particular person I am addressing;

4 I feel I must express only fully formed statements which are binding or that I may sometimes express rambling statements which indicate I am searching for more adequate and precise expressions;

5 I am certain of most of the components involved or am hesitant because of what I think of myself, think of the subject or the circumstances I am in — or was in, when what I am talking about happened;

6 I have the proper vocabulary;

7 I have the right to speak of this subject at the moment;

8 my image of myself is that of a shy person, a charmer, or of one needing to make the best impression possible in the circumstances;

9 the purpose motivating my verbal expression is to compromise or to be responsible for making some

definite impact on those who need to know exactly what I think or what they can expect from me?

10 I must find a way to extricate myself from a difficult situation?

Of course, we shall all find ourselves in such situations on one day or another. But do we take time to prepare a list like the one above for the purpose of knowing how wide is the spectrum of our verbal expression?

To become aware of all the above will take care of much that I need to know about myself as someone who is contemplating writing as a mode of expression. In fact, I can become a "virtual writer" first and do all that work on the oral plane: and it may extend over several hours of daily encounters with people.

I can design this oral exercise for my self: describe to myself

1 every person I am familiar with,

2 every object I set my eyes upon,

3 every field of vision that affects my open eyes,

4 and in particular, those persons or things I find pleasing, those which strike me as odd, those that repel me, those I want to get involved with, etc. . .

and see for how long I can entertain any or all, in which ways and to what extent, and to which level of precision and accuracy.

These oral tasks will convey to me not only that I have lots to say, but that I can give expression and expressions a reality and objectivity which will permit me to work on them and achieve self-imposed goals and targets.

Do I know how my moods affect my verbal expressions?

For instance, is being *sad* itself a selector of certain components of my speech which convey to me and others that this is my mood? No doubt, I can conclude from hearing a voice on the phone that the speaker is sad and confirm my guess through the words I hear. I must know inside myself what it is to be sad in order to extend it to others, and this helps me to know how others feel their sadness and what testimonies they give outsiders. Such searching does two things; it makes me know something about myself, and that I and others have corresponding inner moods and tendencies. I therefore know more than myself and in this way secure an entry into others as they do into me.

Can I make people laugh by telling them some words in certain ways? Do I know something of the comic side of life, and can I use it to generate gaiety in others through statements I make with words specially selected by me.

Do I find it easier to make people feel sad rather than delighted; or the other way round? Do I not have many opportunities to study the role of words chosen specifically to create a release of tension that may reach the level of an explosion of laughter?

Can I specialize in telling jokes?

Can I study the jokes of others to find out why they may make one "crack up" and apply my findings in generating my own jokes?

Do I remember jokes? Which ones? For how long? What makes me want to tell them, and on which occasions?

Can I sense that all statements have, associated with them, an affective component which allows us to classify them as: matter of fact, comic, dramatic, sad, suspenseful, mysterious, thrilling, unlikely or common, exceptional, erotic, subversive, shameful, dreadful or unbecoming, out of place, intimate, titillating, and so forth. Where do we find each component and how do we put it in our statements to obtain particular results when we want them? There are so many occasions for us to come in contact with this affective component that some of us discover very young which words to use for irritating our parents and siblings.

Sarcasm and irony are less reachable through the written word than through the voice because it must be modulated in a certain way to produce the required impact. The exclamation mark after a word, like "Beautiful!" is a poor conveyor of what is felt by a disgusted person who exclaims it. Hence irony is not as easily detected in a printed passage as from the same words spoken out. Writers can get away with some of their subversive statements (as DeFoe and Swift did centuries ago) by using the subterfuge of irony to hide what they think and give different impressions to the censors who can thus be fooled.

By concentrating on such matters we are telling our students that becoming a writer is open to all of us provided we learn to pay attention to a number of facts of life, and of awareness present in our multifarious expressions as they occur every day in all of our lives. For some, more often than for others.

If there are incomparably more speakers than there are writers, it is mainly because a general awareness — that we all say lots of things and therefore know that we have something to say — had escaped us, and specific awarenesses which can be picked up — of the various connections between words and moods or thoughts or feelings etc. — have not become for most of us part of our ordinary activity.

In this encounter with the future writer in us, we have stressed the education of awareness and conveyed that this must take place in the proper areas and manners so as to end up resulting in the education of the writer in each of us. We can all become writers provided we pay the price and, to begin with, there is the cost of being aware of ourselves as speakers and observers, noting the power of words and their effect — the effect of our own words on others, and of their words on ourselves — in a multitude of human settings.

As youngsters we experienced the fascination of stories: those of fairies and gods, for the older among us; those of space adventure and space wars, for the younger. We have made our visual imagination readier to respond by watching TV but we have blunted our hearing by too much noise. We know that our lives extend to imaginary worlds and we entertain a number of them — getting great satisfaction from this. Our practical life, more often than not, seems dull and we escape from it in so many ways through our imagination. Being aware of this too will help us meet the future writer in us.

12 What Kind of Writer Can I Be

Teachers who want to help their students to find the answer to the question above will be better served when they give their students a sufficient number of exercises so that their knowledge of themselves as writers may emerge more clearly.

In fact, common sense tells us that writing, like digesting, can only be done by oneself. Hence, if we give our students a wide range of writing experiences, so that they can examine carefully which type of writing meets with their temperaments, stamina, imaginations, and circumstances, then we shall make a proper contribution to their education as writers. They are the ones who must choose where they feel most at home, at ease and most involved and able to pursue their own careers as writers most adequately and happily — even if it is a second career, or a side career, or even a virtual career never to be known publicly.

We may find a place for ourselves in helping our students by looking with them at their productions and, through this, leading them to find their own criteria for assessing their work.

But, we can do even more for them if we let the other members of their class examine the work and express their views and their justifications of these. In a way, in terms of education, this is more economical than teacher "correction." Indeed, doing the study in the open enables all the class to use the same duration to learn a certain number of things simultaneously and to convey to each other that there are a number of viewpoints possible on everything. Not least of these is the insight that being fully absorbed in one's viewpoint does not necessarily mean that one's views are based more on fact, and it becomes understandable that one's critics may have views that differ. Another by-product may be: more objectivity in front of our own work and the development of the capacity for self-criticism, thus helping us to avoid disappointment when our efforts are poorly received.

To explain the "more" that can be done for the students we shall resort to a presentation of our work with people that has gone on for more than twenty years. Working with people of different ages and in intensive seminars — using different languages on various occasions — we have gathered a considerable experience which is now summarized in this chapter.

* * *

Our common-sense-of-writing-classes differ considerably from each other. Their function has not been to develop a foolproof approach to writing which can be generalized and promoted, but to bring out what the education of the writer in oneself actually means and what it entails.

Sometimes, the first exercise is used not as an actual example to study but rather to convey that we shall be actively writing all through the course. It stems from questions like these: "What do I expect from this workshop?" or "What made me register for a writing workshop?" or "Do I know what I want from being here?" and is to be answered in writing. The participants are told to take 10 or 15 minutes to put down their answers.

Even if they expect that their writings will be considered in one way or another, they are not. The seminar leader has had those same minutes to watch the participants while they were writing to note: whether some hesitated a lot in starting while others at once plunged into stringing words on paper; whether some wrote at length and then erased or crossed out their sentences while others wrote, read, corrected, and wrote further, etc.

While watching the class, if the leader finds the time given seems too short for too many then a few more minutes are added. Otherwise, the exercise is considered over and the leader asks questions about what happened *not* about what was written.

1 did anyone feel that this number of minutes had been spent on writing?

2 did anyone find in considering the question that one was thrown back into oneself: first, to find the inner climate necessary to meet the question, then to gather the items needed, and then to sort them out in order to put them down on paper? (Sometimes a vigil in oneself is encountered and known as a judge that censors or passes the items and their verbal correspondents.)

3. did anyone feel: "*I* am writing" or "I *am* writing" or "I am *writing*!" or was everyone totally engrossed in the act of answering the question?

4. did anyone think about the fact that the other participants were facing the same question? Were they expecting very similar answers or exclusively individual ones?

Once the workshop people realize that we are not going to make their statements public, some are disappointed while others are relieved. They are told that the exercise is over as far as this workshop is concerned, since it aimed at starting us off and seeing that writing can take place even when provoked by a benign casual question.

In this way, everyone discovers that getting us to write is not difficult. In fact, during the remaining hours, participants may be given occasions for reading to the group from those first statements when it is needed to make any of their cases clearer.

* * *

From what was mentioned in the previous chapter, it is clear that a workshop leader cannot feel lacking in subject matter suitable for writing exercises. But are there "roadblocks" the leader must carefully avoid? Since it is not known why people register, who they are, and where they are on their road to the mastery of writing, one of the blocks to avoid is represented by the masses of emotional energy that can be triggered by questions related to psychic and affective matters.

Because of this, we then work on transmuting into words one's direct perception of some object from the outside. Either we choose a specific object to be placed in front of the class such as a box which we can open or keep closed or the microphone used for audiotaping the workshop; or (if we think it appropriate) we can suggest writing about one's hands or one of one's thumbs.

Any writer will soon note that one's perception is not that pure; that associations draw our attention and make pure description of objects as difficult as pure perception of them. This much we learn about the writer and writing.

The duration given to this exercise may be revised, either by stopping the exercise earlier since most participants have put down their pens, or by extending it when more time is clearly needed by a number of the writers.

On this occasion there is a good reason to ask all students to read aloud what they have put down. Everyone sees the object written about or recalls what specific object was suggested as a topic (one's hand or thumb), and we can learn:

1 how differently the same task was tackled by the various participants, and

2 how the "intrinsic properties" of the object affect the different people.

It often helps to let listeners shut their eyes so they can better concentrate on the words they are hearing.

There may be some of the texts read which require immediate feedback from those who are listening, but it may as easily happen that a general feedback session after all the readings are completed serves best the needs of the group.

Valuable learnings can follow from this session:

1 that so much talent is available in this group and may therefore be found in any randomly assembled set of people;

2 that humans are gifted in so many ways which can be spelled out here on the basis of what was heard;

3 that writing descriptions can be fun;

4 that descriptions through associations can spill over into inspired images, striking analogies and contrasts, flights of the imagination, and so forth;

5 that description is a writing genre which can be acquired by duplicating several times the process experienced in that short session;

6 that descriptions may have the attributes of enhancing one's perceptive penetration and one's capacity for observing details — especially those details which count and contribute more to bringing some relief into the picture evoked by the words;

7 that descriptions prepare the ground for a deeper acquaintance with objects and for animating them; and

8 that descriptions are potentially compatible with some other uses of oneself-as-a-writer and may be used for increasing certain impacts on the readers.

Of all the learnings, the most valuable one to emerge is that a number of the participants already feel they can write and feel that they may wish to go on writing even after this workshop.

* * *

Two complementary exercises may follow this work on descriptions. One, is the study of how a short statement can be made into a longish paragraph. This teaches us how to elaborate some items implicit in that statement in order to make it clearer though not necessarily without any confusion, and to reduce the chances of letting one's readers guess too much.

The second exercise is the reverse of the first. Starting with one longish paragraph, can we reduce it again and again; pruning from it all "unnecessary" elements but still maintaining its essential meaning in the final form. This teaches conciseness, compactness in using words, the relative roles of words in statements, and the varying demands of meaning upon the form.

Here too, individual work is alternated with group discussion and general feedback. One learns from what one does and from knowing what was there to be done; all of this is clarified as the contributions of the participants are shared and then discussed.

* * *

As a next step in this work we may ask our group to involve themselves for one session in the writing of telegrams. During this session we discover —

1. that it is possible to omit some words but not others, and
2. that these omitted words are those of the vehicular language and cannot be nouns, quantifiers or certain verbs.

Producing telegrams serves to deepen the sense that the vehicular vocabulary is essentially distinct from the topical vocabulary, and that it dwells in the speakers of that language and is triggered by the apparent structures punctuated by the order of the words retained in the telegrams. These omitted words can be omitted precisely because they can be supplied unambiguously by the readers of the telegram. If the danger of confusion exists, some functional words must be retained.

Such sessions are enjoyed by the participants because in this way they are allowed to make discoveries about their language, their own intelligence regarding it, and their cleverness at work.

* * *

Writing letters takes one or two sessions (each usually lasting around 90 minutes) and covers a whole gamut: from letters to relatives, to friends, to a special person one loves, to letters introducing oneself to one's advantage, or serving as circulars extolling the qualities of one's product (whether an invention, a project, a proposal of various reforms, etc.), or inviting someone to become a partner, a follower, or a fellow-traveler, and so forth.

The fact that letters can be as short as one wants and yet never too long, may entice people to take the pen and write. There are no prescribed formats for the content of letters and this latitude is helpful in encouraging some people to write.

The feedback sessions are usually extremely valuable. The participants manage to show their sense of humor, and also their special brand of imagination both in the choice of subject and in its treatment. Generally, the group comes out of such a session excited and desirous to give to letter writing an expanded place in their lives. This of course makes a contribution to keeping the morale of the workshop even higher than before.

There are several factors that affect letter writing: the qualities of intimacy — that is, expressions of affection, tenderness, love — and those of formality of different kinds determined by the social function or position of the person addressed; the laisser faire or rigor permitted this person; the selection of whom one is writing to; even the degree of sensitivity or perceptiveness of the writer about what has been chosen for reporting — whether it is personal, familiar, bordering on indiscretion, and so on. All of this is revealed in letter writing and thus confirms Buffon's statement: "Le style c'est l'homme" (or "everyone betrays oneself in one's style of writing"). This is truer of letters than of other writings, although there too, this also happens.

Letter writing is a recognized literary genre. Writing and studying several types of letters at a workshop is good preparation for entry into the collected letters of famous people.

* * *

Writing jokes — carried out as a special study of how one generates in a few words a convulsion of laughter in one's readers — is another exercise. In fact, a session spent on writing jokes can have much more impact on the participants than some of the other sessions. Because most people think first of jokes they have heard and are more inclined to tell these jokes than create their own, they usually fail to ask themselves whether they are capable of such creation and whether jokes have specific attributes which give them their own place in literature. When these questions are asked of the participants it becomes possible to discover that almost all of us are endowed with the quality of mind which allows us to see "the funny" where it is, and that it is perhaps almost everywhere.

By analyzing some of the jokes produced on the spot, we can note that laughter is due to a jolt from meeting the unexpected — something which most of us prefer to banish from our minds. A shaggy-dog story takes advantage of this tendency by leading the listeners or readers along a most ordinary path up to the last moment when the unexpected is brought in through the last few words.

In contrast, one-liners select words which at once shatter attitudes held consciously or unconsciously by the listeners, due to either the characters or personalities involved, or the events and situations referred to. The comic effect can be great or slight, depending on the ease with which the balance of our conscious expectations in the situation is upset. Our preconceptions and prejudices form the scaffoldings of our potential for thinking about most common things, and hence we do get jolted when what we hear or see does not fall into the prerequisites assumed to obtain in such situations. For example, we expect a walking person not to do anything but go on walking and then if he falls, this at once provokes a laughter rather than pity (although this may appear later).

Sometimes, through a session on jokes people discover a new talent in themselves which they may continue to exploit.

* * *

Writing biographical sketches and portraits may generate a further set of exercises.

What is suggested is that we attempt to find out if there is in us a coalescing of words by the mere evocation of a certain person we know well. For example: one of our parents, some close relative or friend we have known for some time, one or another of our many teachers, or certain of our colleagues.

If we select writing about a person in an actual setting we have known well, we enter into a biographical sketch. If we write about the person outside any special frame of reference, in order to gloss over the attributes which we associate with this person, we enter into a portrait.

In order to begin we suggest the following game: each one is to write a few paragraphs inspired by any one present in the room, and then as each writing is read aloud the challenge is to figure out which one of us has served as the model.

At the same time as we work on portraying people (whether cursorily on brief acquaintance or in-depth after having known them for some time), we are working on "the art of portraying." Clearly, the clumsy sketches will distract and keep us guessing while those well etched will lead us straight to the person and make us appreciate that person as well as the artist.

The immensity of the field and the variety of people in the world around us will show us that we can go on indefinitely with such exercises and collect a portfolio of written sketches which can one day serve us if we want to create either short stories or full-size novels.

Literature is full of portraits and we recommend, after working one oneself to produce some, that we turn to books and see how famous writers have done this job. It can become a fascinating study which leads us to sensitize ourselves to others and to seeing them as either cast in marble or made of an infinite number of impressionistic touches all in hues and nuances.

These exercises, while teaching us about writing, teach us about being and about all the possibilities of being. They teach us to appreciate the reality of the absence of type among humans — making room for all sorts of characters such as those caught by playwrights or novelists — and letting us know the value of variety as against the monotonous repetition of statified types. At the least they will keep us alert in the presence of other human beings, since no one can really guess who is behind the mask or form we see with our eyes. If we can write of what we see, can we attempt to go beyond this and venture what may be in store if we become intimately acquainted with some of those who cross our field of vision?

* * *

The short story and the novel are genres which allow us to delve into these more extensive studies. Unfortunately, these works demand much more time than the exercises we can accommodate in our workshops. Still, we can give a taste of this expansion in writing by making the participants feel that they wish they could have more time to take one or another of their characters beyond what they have so far portrayed. To get people to experience a *thirst for writing* may be as important as to give them a tour of the genres of literature.

If we achieve this in so few hours, we can claim that we have managed to come close to understanding how to help people to become writers although we know that only by writing and writing and writing will they acquire the craft.

The affective component here must also be brought to the fore. Humans can have a project and stop at this. But, if they have stamina, patience, a deep motivation to take something further and further until the moment *it* says: "I am done, you can stop here," they will know to what extent a literary work is representative of oneself.

One can climb the steps of the stairs which lead to the "monument" of literature by finding at each stage whether one's intellectual and affective qualities can support one's imagination and one's endeavor at literary creation. Writing a letter or a short passage may be all one can manage and yet one can make both into chiseled diamonds. A succession of integrated letters or passages may result in a jewel made of diamonds and yet not be a diamond itself. Whether or not the jewel still keeps its appeal as the diamonds do, will reveal whether or not one has promoted oneself to the rank of short-story writer or novelist.

* * *

Poetry is another genre we can incorporate in our exercises for making people reach the *writer* in them.

During their adolescence, some people may have tried to write some poems but now have stopped even contemplating doing so. Thus, to motivate the participants at a workshop, we create a tension in them by asking that a free poem be written on a most unpoetic topic such as "my mother's sewing machine," or "the nail of my right thumb," or "the cigarette butt in the ashtray," or "the undissolved sugar at the bottom of my teacup," and so on.

Invariably this "clash" has proved very fruitful for a number of participants in several workshops. A few add to the challenge of making lines rhyme, even if this is not considered as part of the definition of a poem.

After listening to the volunteers read their poems, it is possible to ask for some attempts at analyzing the qualities of a poem. All know intuitively what a poem is as it is being read, even if they cannot reach a clear definition of it. There are elements of incantation which are not present in other literary genres, and our affectivity is moved in manners which confirm the unique powers of the genre.

* * *

While one is preparing participants for writing short stories one can consider aspects of writing that may one day lead them to writing novels. For instance, it is possible to merge a number of the impacts from previous exercises and then to discuss the possibilities of expanding a short text into a much more extensive one. The latter may require time, stamina, a strong memory of all that has been written in pages preceding the ones being worked on at this moment. A vast imagination supported by a sense of reality is needed to manipulate a group of characters acting in conjunction yet in a variety of situations. A critical sense of pruning is required not only of material written, but even of ideas present before the writing has taken shape. The fatal result of inadequate pruning is one which generates boredom in the reader, and it is to be as carefully avoided as that unevenness which betrays a lack of readiness to write more than short passages.

In addition, good short passages by themselves may have as much to give readers as they do when integrated to form a larger work. Writers will have to be content with finding the genres that suit them and their circumstances, unless they are willing to struggle with themselves in order to overcome weaknesses they recognize in themselves. But they may have to learn that readers do not have to be used in order for them to find out their weaknesses.

It can be helpful to write a paragraph (or two) as to look at what one has written in order to examine if its germ has a place in future writing. Since in this procedure the stress is on the potential for expansion, we enter into this text differently than we do when we want only to appreciate the literary qualities of the original as was stressed in previous exercises. For the education of the writers, we do together, deliberately and systematically, what every writer can do when rereading one of one's short passages at a later date — finding in it some points which stimulate one to revise and expand one's work or make one discard it.

In a short workshop on writing, in which many tasks are tackled, we must exclude undertaking a study of those qualities required for writing novels. Here we may only spend one session examining from a distance what we know of the way of working of recognized novelists already read by several participants. This has some usefulness.

It may come as a shock that great writers (like Honoré de Balzac, George Sand, Emile Zola and many less great prolific ones) wrote their novels at one stretch — writing for many hours during the day and night — while others (among them, Gustave Flaubert and Henry James) sweated out their novels page-by-page working carefully on each sentence and rarely being completely satisfied. The outcomes of both ways of working are admirable, yet each of these writers admired only the way of working which seemed to them unreachable. The part temperament plays in achieving monumental novels keeps us breathless, puts us in our place. The Tolstoys, Dostoevskis, Zolas and Prousts have imitators who rarely manage to do more than fill longer sagas — an obvious tribute to imitators' stamina and their many other qualities, but still showing the lack of *genius* characterizing the great novelists.

Living in contact with great writers — while teaching us so much about art and literature — can also teach us how to find our place and be the kind of writer that is compatible with *our* mental and affective gifts. In this way we can direct our ambitions appropriately.

* * *

Writing in this section of the book has been treated solely as part of the literary use of words. But words are also the medium of scientists, advertisers in news publications, textbook writers, journalists, and speech writers. Some of the qualities encountered in the above exercises will be required for all these types of writing — especially clarity, conciseness, correctness and so forth which affect expression and can help verbal communication.

Common sense can help us consider afresh the challenges offered by the preparation of all these types of writers, but we cannot take this up in this much more restricted work.

Postword

This text has been on the workbench for eight or nine years. The part on writing was completed last, two years ago. The delay in publication is due to the uncertainty that the body of teachers of reading and writing were ready to entertain the propositions in the text. Although commonsensical, as far as we are concerned, we preferred to obtain signs that it would be welcome by a sufficient number of students of the teaching of language arts, to justify its appearing as a book. Now we have these signs and therefore we decided to send it to the printers to appear early in 1985.

It is one more volume in the series *"The Common Sense of Teaching. . ."* which represents the translation of the findings of the *Science of Education* into terms valid for the classroom teacher and guaranteeing success in the places where most children learn to read and write, arithmetic, foreign languages, and other subject matters.

Though addressed to the teachers who earn their living working in classrooms and polarized so as to give them as much help as possible, the contents will be of use to all students of teaching, whether psychologists, sociologists, epistemologists or ad-administrators, wanting to find a real basis for an actual solution of the challenge of literacy and of writing, in countries where education is free and compulsory.

We hope users of this book will feel the impulse to let us know to what extent it has been helpful in their special case. Writing for the public means writing for unknown people. Readers can change that by sending us a personal letter and letting us benefit from their experience as we hope they did from ours. We thank, in advance, those who will accept that invitation and assist us in providing the evidence we need to have to state that we have made a contribution to the practice of education.

C.G.

Appendix A:
Black and White Charts

Content of the *Word Charts*

Analysis of the *Word Charts*

Content of the *English Language Fidel*

Key to the *English Language Fidel*

pat pit pet pot
pop at it up putt
tot top tip tap apt
as pep us pup is
-s sat sit set sap -s
's stop step spot 's
stops steps pass pest
sips tess tests past
puppet asset

1

mat tim met tom mom
must mumps mast l
mops miss mess pump
a am stamps map sum
sam pam not nut
net ten man men 'm
tent spent sent pants
pin sun an in on son
tempt attempt assistant

2

fan fun of fist fit
if fat stuff puff -y
dad mad and dud dust
tennis sniff did mend
sad stand end this -ed
mud sand that fed -ed
them then than the -ed
yes fifth yam fifty yet
thin independent path

3

let doll dull sell tell
lit land less spell lot
lap lend lent pal -es
until ill mill still
last plus add slept
tummy daddy funny -i-
wit wet with will 'll
swim was well went
wind sunset else wind

4

ran rat after run rust
red sister rest strip
my mind wild mine ask
kit kill kid kiss any
skip skill silk milk
sick neck track truck
dress strike find -ly
time mile like love -d
fur were word world -d

5

hot has him her his hat
back do brick to black
two impossible too 've
father zoo mother -ing
food little work have
took full put look -n't
sorry worry been move
five by brother but give
from there won't don't

6

hate date late male 're
more for or nor horse
take same made fatal
be we me he the here
bone woke nose home
seven no go so iron -e-
use refuse united cute
girl bursts hurt first
egg got globe get leg

7

month thank think both
sold bankrupt told
come done gone some
hungry cold hundred
dirty thirty thirsty -er
hand off april dog -est
simple hope promise
lost difficult most
goes able big open does

8

shop shut chin she ship
chill china teach chips
wish push share cash
match much such watch
shell front shock shall
child channel children
far very are close car
michigan every chorus
hair ever air even pair

9

small chicken school
church cry all shred
schedule gym criminal
false adjective call
soldier box neither
judge next act job
education generation
potato crime tomorrow
orchestra ate character

10

phrase garden which
question quiet quickly
capable seen once one
blood fantastic see door
your you mouth young
foot sleep while feet
these between those
why what where when
since whom who whose

11

physics how elephant
photograph now courage
hour out soup our house
four courageous low fore
tooth could about teeth
should shoulder would
be- cause gun side busy
worse sugar better wood
sure good hind age want

12

eyes high height lie
night saturday might
under money above down
paid honey prayers mail
may finished field way
stopped conceit rolled
talk vision says walk
they day say greyhound
received england family

13

eighth eighteen eighty
freight wrong fright
list listen few news
fast fasten lesson heir
sword business sworn
know knee new knew
dumb buy said dye again
right written true write
soul knowledge -tieth

14

ear hear tear theater
read heart heard read
eat believe sieve friend
receipt meant seize
great please vein gauge
pear create ocean tear
pearl their means break
anxiety treasure anxious
exaggerate examination

15

during autumn daughter
pure taught water poor
doubt awe oh saw sore
tough laugh soar cough
thought through though
bough thoroughly help
board sew sow bored
cloak broke clock sow
sweet fruit suit suite

16

isle loaves calves aisle
number loaf half flown
woman flowers women
boy zero zip dizzy buoy
thursday oil wednesday
ghost diaphragm psalm
rhythm mission rhyme
key ah tissue sign quay
khaki ache schism waltz

17

hallelujah pneumatic
champion venture million
queue life jewel view
toward bathe awkward
pension clothes amoeba
often aerial shoes build
pigeon different mayor
special budget spatial
science equals straight

18

except exhibit accept
garage appreciate length
language conscientious
handkerchief humanity
chocolate asia cupboard
hymn mnemonic beauty
foreign heifer shepherd
ballet sapphire plague
leopard finesse machine

19

guest guarantee tongue
bury stranger choir debt
medical acquire medicine
rogue blackguard signify
precious argue luxurious
asthma cassette azure
ancient certain student
direct direction distance
office exhaust official

20

Analysis Of The *Word Charts*

CHART	NEW SOUNDS	NEW SPELLINGS	WORD PARTS
1	a (at), u (up), e (pet) i (it), e (puppet), o (pot) p, pp, t, tt, s (is), s (us), ss (pass)		-s (pets) -s (tens) 's (pat's) 's (sam's)
2	a (a mess), I (I am) m, n	o (son)	'm (I'm)
3	f (if), f (of), y (yes) d, th (this), th (thin)	e(independent) , o (of) y(fifty) nn, ff	-y (puffy) -ed (fanned) -ed (puffed) -ed (mended)
4	l, ll, w 'll (I' ll)	i (wind, mind) a (was), u (until) mm, dd, se (else)	-i - (funnier) -es (passes) 'll (I' ll)
5	r, re(were), k, ck, ke(like) u (fur), e (were), o (word)	y (my), a (any), me(time) l (wild), le(mile), ve(love), ne(mine)	-d(loved) -d(liked) -ly(likely)
6	a(father), o(won't), e(there) o(to), oo(too), wo(two), oo(took), u(put), h, b, ng(ing)	ee (been) rr (sorry) z (zoo)	've (I've) -n't(haven't) -ing (willing)
7	a(late) , o(or), e(he), u(use) g(go) , gg(egg) r(iron), re(here)	i(girl), v (seven), se(nose) on(iron), c (cute) te(late) be(globe), de(made),	-e- 're(we're)
8	o(off)	oe(goes), oe(does) n(think), pe(hope)	-er(wilder) -est(wildest)
9	sh, ch(michigan) ch(chin)	a(share), ai(air), ea(teach) ch(chorus)	
10	j, g(gym), d(soldier) dj (adjective), dge(judge) x (box)	a(all), ei(neither), ie(soldier), o(tomorrow) ow(tomorrow), t(education)	
11	o(one), ou(mouth) you (your), qu(quickly)	ee (see), oo (door) you, oo(blood), ou (young) ph(phrase), t(question) wh(which), wh(who), ce(once)	
13	s(vision)	NOTE: *Except for the few sounds noted, Charts 12-20 introduce* ***only*** *new spellings.*	
15	x(anxious), x(examination)		
17	m(rhythm)		
20	x(luxurious)		

Appendix A:
Black and White Charts

a, au, ai, i
u, o, a, ou, oo, oe
i, o, a, u, e, ia, ie, ea, ae, is
y, ey, ay, ee, ai, ei, hi, hea, ois
e, ea, a, u, ai, ay, ie, eo, ei, ae
o, a, ho, oh, ow, eau
a, u, i, io, iou, eou, ia, ie, au, ea, ah, he
e, o, ou, oi, oa, eo, ai, ei, iu, eau, ough, y
u, e, o, i, ea, ou, y
o, a, au, aw, awe, ough, oa, augh, oo, ou, hau, ho, ao, oi, owa
a, ea, ah, aa, au, e
o, oo, ew, ou, ui, u, oe, ue, eu, ough, wo, ieu
e, ee, ea, y, ie, ei, i, eo, ey, ay, oe, ae, is
a, ai, ea, e, ei, hei, ae, aye, ayo, ey
oo, ou, u, o | u, eu, ue
o, a, au, oa, oo, ou, ho, ao, oi, owa
I, i, y, ie, ye, igh, eye, eigh, is, ais, ei, aye
a, ai, ay, ey, ei, eigh, ea, aigh, et, ae, au, e, ee
o, oe, ow, owe, oa, ou, ew, oh, ough, eau, oo, au, eo, ot
u, ew, iew, eau, ue, ieu, ewe, hu, eu, eue
ou, hou, ow, ough | oi, oy, aw | oi | o

p, pp, pe, ph, bp
t, tt, te, ed, d, tte, pt, bt, ct, cht, th, phth, 't | z, zz
s, ss, se, 's, z, zz, ze, x, si, thes, sth, s' | 's
s, ss, se, 's, c, ce, sc, st, sw, ps, sce, sse, sth, z
s, z, ge, t
m, mm, me, mb, lm, gm, mn, 'm | m
n, nn, ne, kn, gn, pn, mn, gne, in, on, dne, nd, ln | n
f, ff, fe, ph, gh, lf, ft, ffe, pph
v, f, ve, lve, ph, 've
d, dd, de, ed, ld, 'd, t, tt
th, the
th, the, h, t, phth
y, i, j, u
l, ll, le, lle, 'll | l, le, 'll
w, wh, u, o | wh
k, kk, ke, ck, c, cc, ch, lk, qu, que, che, cqu, cch, co, kh
r, rr, re, wr, rh, rps, rp, rt, rrh, rre, lo, 're | r, re, 're
b, bb, be, bu, pb
h, wh, j
g, gg, gu, gh, gue, ckgu
sh, ch, t, s, ss, c, sch, sc, che, chs
ch, tch, t, c, che
ng, n, ngue, nd
j, g, d, dge, ge, gg, dg, dj
qu, cqu
x, xe, cc, xc | x | x | x

American English Fidel

Key to the English language Fidel

buff	pale yellow	pink	blue	white	yellow
a — at au — laugh ai — plaid i — meringue	u — up o — done a — was ou — young oo — blood oe — does	i — it o — women a — village u — busy e — english ia — marriage ie — sieve ea — guinea ae — caesarian is — chassis y — beauty ey — honey ay — saturday ui — build ee — been ai — portrait ei — forfeit hi — exhibit hea — forehead ois — chamois	e — pet ea — lead a — any u — bury ai — said ay — says ie — friend eo — leopard ef — heifer ae — aesthetic	o — pot a — swamp ho — honor oh — john ow — knowledge eau — bureaucracy	a — usable u — upon i — possible io — question iou — anxious eou — righteous ia — martial ie — conscience au — restaurant ea — pageant ah — hallelujah he — vehement

turquoise	moss	pale pink/moss	brown	white/pale pink	blue/pale pink
a — care ai — air ea — pear e — there ei — their hei — heir ae — aerial aye — prayers ayo — mayor ey — they're	oo — look ou — would u — put o — woman	u — cure you — your eu — europe	o — or a — war au — dinosaur oa — board oo — door ou — pour ho — exhort ao — extraordinary *oi — reservoir owa — toward	I — I i — like y — my ie — lie ye — dye igh — high eye — eyes eigh — height is — isle ais — aisle * ei — either aye — aye	a — late ai — mail ay — day ey — they ei — vein eigh — eight ea — great aigh — straight et - ballet ae — israeli au — gauge e — suede ee — fiancee

dark brown	magenta	lilac	yellow/lilac	lime	cobalt blue	tangerine	yellow/tangerine	lavender	yellow/lavender
p — pot pp — stopped pe — hope ph — Shepherd bp — subpoena	t - top tt — little te — late ed — finished d — placed tte — cigarette pt — receipt bt — debt ct — indict cht — yacht th — thyme phth — phthisic 't — don't	s — is ss — scissors se — hose 's — pam's z — zoo zz — dizzy ze — seize x — anxiety si — business thes — clothes sth — asthma	's — james's	s — us ss — pass se — promise 's — pat's c — receipt ce — once sc — science st — listen sw — sword ps — psalm sce — aquiesce sse — finesse sch — schism sth — isthmus z — waltz	s — measure z — azure ge — garage t — equation	m — mat mm — comma me — same mb — lamb lm — calm gm — diaphragm mn — hymn 'm — I'm	m — rhythm	n — in nn — funny ne — fine kn — know gn — sign pn — pneumatic mn — mnemonic gne — champagne in — extraordinary on — iron dne — wednesday nd — grandfather ln — lincoln	n — wouldn't

pale aqua	pale blue/pale aqua	gold	orange	yellow/orange	dark green	pale blue	gray
w - wet wh — when u — suite o — choir	*wh — where	k — kiss kk — trekked ke — like ck — sick c — cat cc — occur ch — chorus lk — talk qu — quay que — clique che — ache cqu — lacquer cch — saccharine co — chocolate kh — khaki	r — ran rr — horror re — more wr — write rh — rhythm rps — corps rp — corpsman rt — mortgage rrh — catarrh rre — bizarre lo — colonel 're — you're	r — iron re — fire 're — we're	b - bay bb — ribbon be — cube bu — buy pb — raspberry	h — hat wh — who j — jose	g - go gg — egg gu — guard gh — ghost gue — league ckgu — blackguard

* Alternate pronunciation

Appendix A: Black and White Charts

yellow	bright pink	ochre	purple	leaf green	red
e — the	u — fur	o — off	a — far	o — do	e — we
o — conceit	o — her	a — all	ea — heart	oo — too	ee — see
ou — numerous	o — work	au — paul	ah — ah	ew — new	ea — tea
oi — turtoise	i — girl	aw — paw	aa — bazaar	ou — soup	y — fifty
oa — cupboard	ea — pearl	awe — awe	*au — laugh	ui — fruit	ie — field
eo — pigeon	ou — courtesy	ough — thought	e — sergeant	u — flu	ei — conceit
ai — captain	y — myrrh	oa — broad		oe — shoe	i — ski
ei — foreign		augh — daughter		ue — blue	eo — people
iu — nasturtium		* oo — floor		eu — pneumatic	ey — key
eau — bureaucrat		ou — cough		ough — through	ay — quay
ough — thoroughly		hau — exhaust		wo — two	oe — amoeba
y — ethyl		* ho — exhort		ieu — lieutenant	ae — aegis
		* ao — extraordinary			is — debris
		* oi — reservoir			
		*owa — toward			

brown/pale aqua	pale pink/leaf green	purple/pale aqua	ochre/rale pink
o — go	u — use	ou — house	oi — oil
oe — goes	you — youth	hou — hour	oy — boy
ow — know	ew — few	ow — sow	* aw — lawyer
owe — owe	iew — view	ough — bough	
oa — joan	eau — beauty		
ou — soul	ue — hue	**pale aqua/purple**	**pale aqua/pale yellow**
ew — sew	ieu — adieu	oi — reservoir	o — one
oh — oh	ewe — ewe		
ough — though	yew — yew		
eau — plateau	hu — exhume		
oo — brooch	eu — feudal		
au — mauve	eue — queue		
eo — yeoman			
ot — depot			

mauve	khaki	green	maroon	pale lime	pale pink	royal blue
f — if	v — seven	d — dust	th — this	th — thin	y — yes	l — let
ff — off	f — of	dd — sudden	the — bathe	the — absinthe	i — onion	ll — sell
fe — life	ve — give	de — made		h — eighth	j — hallelujah	le — pale
ph — photograph	lve — halves	ed — rolled		t — southampton	u — vacuum	lle — gazelle
gh — cough	ph — stephen	ld — would		phth — phthalein		'll — he'll
lf — half	've — I've	'd — I'd				**yellow/royal blue**
ft — often		* t — water				l — wild
ffe — giraffe		*tt — butter				le — simple
pph — sapphire						'll — I'll

sky blue	dark magenta	olive	green/cobalt blue	gold/pale aqua	gold/lime
sh — she	ch — chin	ng — sing	j — jack	qu — quickly	x — box
ch — machine	tch — watch	n — bankrupt	g — gem	cqu — acquiesce	xe — axe
t — education	t — question	ngue — tongue	d — soldier		cc — accept
s — sugar	c — cello	nd — handkerchief	dge — judge		xc — excel
ss — tissue	che — niche		ge — cage		**gray/lilac**
c — appreciate			gg — exaggerate		x — exist
sch — schist			dg — judgment		**gold/sky blue**
sc — conscience			dj — adjective		x — anxious
che — cache					**gray/cobalt blue**
					x — luxurious

Appendix B:
List of Materials

Classroom and Student Materials*

Needed to work out step-by-step the proposals in Chapters 3-6:

- Colored classroom charts (16" × 22")

    Content same as shown in Appendix A.

    - *20 Word Charts* for Visual Dictation #2
    - *Fidel* (or 8 Phonic Code Charts)

        For Visual Dictation #1

        For study of spelling

    - *Sound/color Rectangle Fidel* (1 chart)

    Available for individual student and teacher use:

    - *Mini Word Charts* (2½" × 3½" — 4 per card)

---

* Editor's Note: Current offerings may vary.

- *Mini Fidel* (5½" × 8" card)
- *Mini Rectangle Fidel* (5½" × 8" card)

- Colored chalks

  For Visual Dictation #1 which introduces "R_0" and Charts 1 and 2

- Collapsible pointer

  For implementing Visual Dictations

- Primer Books

  R_0 *the discipline of reading*

  R_1 *the first certificate of reading*

  R_2 *all the sounds of English*

  R_3 *all the spellings of English*

- Book of Stories

  Short stories which can be read separately or considered as a unit because the same family appears in each story (and which also gradually introduce the conventions of English capitalization and punctuation to beginners).

- Worksheets

  - Worksheets 1 - 7

    For use with R_1 and R_2

- Worksheets 8 - 14

  For use with R_3 *and* Book of Stories

  Both sets contain a certain number of games (several explained in this book) which develop awareness of: the dynamic structure of words, spelling, vocabulary, comprehension, and creative writing.

- Short Passages, Eight Tales, and English Worksheets

  These may serve as very useful advanced material for both reading and writing with students of any age.

All of the materials in Appendix B are part of *Words in Color* by C. Gattegno, and are available from Educational Solutions Worldwide Inc., www.EducationalSolutions.com

Additional Teacher Materials

Gattegno, C.

Background and Principles

What We Owe Children

The Universe of Babies

Spelling Kit

Components:

- *Notes for Teachers*
- *Hints* on introducing and using the Fidel
- *Suggested Words and Sentences* to introduce the Fidel

Bernhardt, William

Just Writing

Gallagher, Joan

With the Five Year Olds

Gilbert, Edna

A Way with Words

- A source book of classroom writing games

Murphy, Sister Leonore

Creative Writing

- A log of a first grade teacher

To Perceive and to Write

- Writing after learning to read

Douglas Can't Read

- A case study of a slow learner

Barnaby

- A case study of a child with learning disabilities

Young, Betty

Learning Together

- Report of an elementary school staff

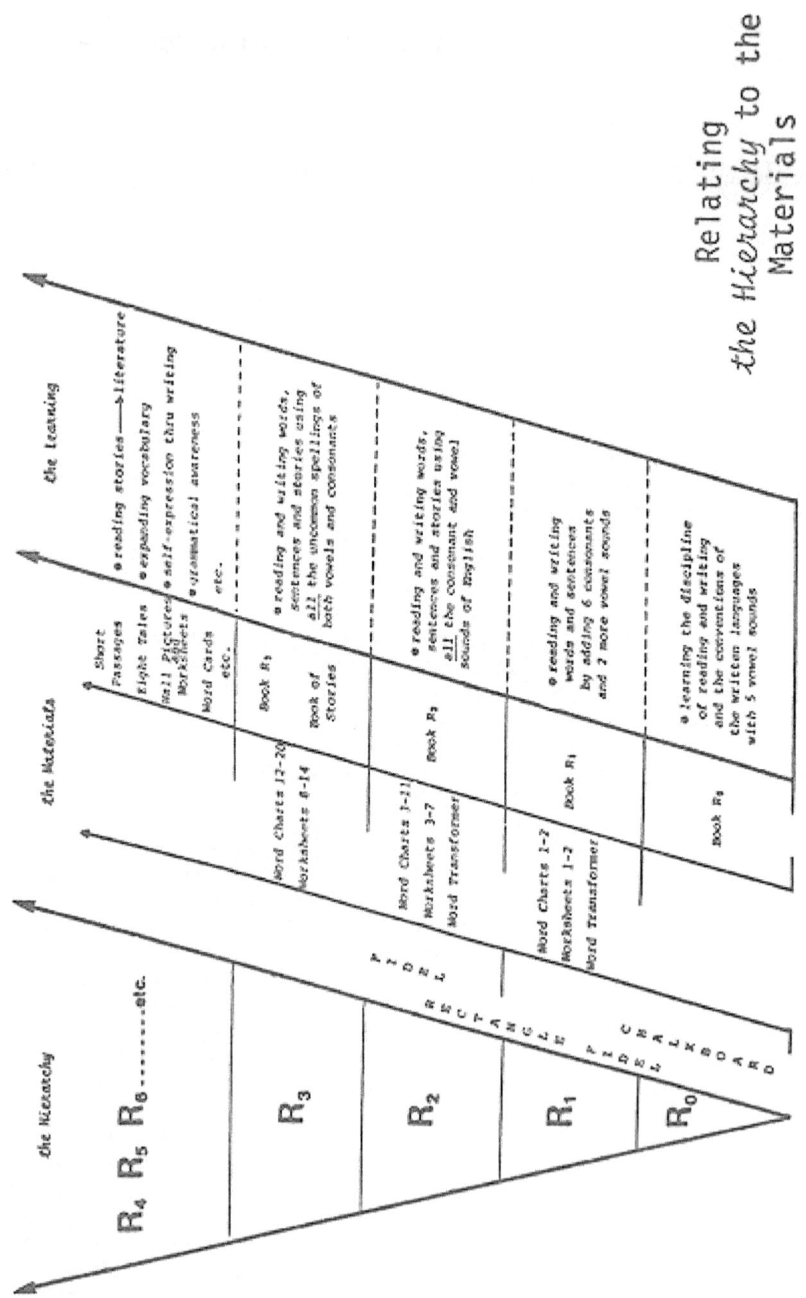
the Hierarchy
R4 R5 R6 ....etc.
R3
R2
R1
R0
RECTANGLE
FIDEL
FIDEL
CHALKBOARD
the Materials
Short Passages
Eight Tales
Wall Pictures and Worksheets
Word Cards etc.
Word Charts 12-20
Worksheets 8-14
Book R3
Book of Stories
Word Charts 3-11
Worksheets 3-7
Word Transformer
Book R2
Word Charts 1-2
Worksheets 1-2
Word Transformer
Book R1
Book R0
the Learning
• reading stories → literature
• expanding vocabulary
• self-expression thru writing
• grammatical awareness
etc.
• reading and writing words, sentences and stories using all the uncommon spellings of both vowels and consonants
• reading and writing words, sentences and stories using all the consonant and vowel sounds of English
• reading and writing words and sentences by adding 6 consonants and 2 more vowel sounds
• learning the discipline of reading and writing and the conventions of the written languages with 5 vowel sounds
Relating
the Hierarchy to the
Materials

www.ingramcontent.com/pod-product-compliance
Lightning Source LLC
LaVergne TN
LVHW061219100826
845148LV00004B/806

* 9 7 8 0 8 7 8 2 5 1 8 4 1 *